The complete book of

vegetable
gardening

The complete book of

vegetable

gardening

From planting to picking –
the complete guide to creating
a bountiful garden

Fern Marshall Bradley
Jane Courtier

Reader's Digest

The Reader's Digest Association, Inc.
London

This edition published by The Reader's Digest Association
by arrangement with Toucan Books, Ltd.

Copyright © 2006 Toucan Books Ltd.

First edition copyright © 2006
The Reader's Digest Association Limited
11 Westferry Circus, Canary Wharf
London E14 4HE

We are committed to both the quality of our products and the service we provide
to our customers. We value your comments, so please feel free to contact us on
08705 113366 or via our web site at: www.readersdigest.co.uk
If you have any comments or suggestions about the content of our books, email
us at: gbeditorial@readersdigest.co.uk

FOR TOUCAN BOOKS
Design: Bradbury and Williams
Editor: Theresa Bebbington
Managing Editor: Ellen Dupont
Editorial Assistant: Maddy Langford
Index: Michael Dent
Picture Research: Christine Vincent, Maria Bembridge
Proofreader: Marion Dent

Front cover photographs: Photolibrary.com Kathryn Kleinman (top left), Garden Picture
Library Friedrich Strauss (top right), Roy Williams (bottom left and right).
Spine photograph: Krivit Photography/Mike Krivit.

A CIP data record for this book is available from the British Library

For more Reader's Digest products and information, visit our website:
www.readersdigest.co.uk

Printed in Singapore

10-digit ISBN 0-276-44088-9
13-digit ISBN 978-0-276-44088-5
Book code 410-052

Part 1: YOUR GARDEN

Part 2: THE VEGETABLES

Introduction

There is something satisfying and rewarding about growing your own food. The sense of achievement when you sit before a plate piled high with fresh produce from your own garden is hard to beat. More gardeners are realising that there is nothing difficult about vegetable growing – and that you don't need an enormous garden to do so.

In Part 1 of *The Complete Book of Vegetable Gardening*, Jane Courtier explains the basics of growing vegetables. There's information to follow from the beginning of the season to the end: how to design a garden that's just the right size and style for your needs; how to improve your soil and prepare it for planting; how to raise seedlings and plant your garden; how to water and feed your crops; how to protect crops from pest and weed problems; how to extend the season; and how to harvest and store all the bounty of your garden.

In Part 2 Fern Marshall Bradley gives you the details on growing specific crops. This section organises

FROM A (MOSTLY) ORGANIC GARDENER

Dear Reader,

I prefer to garden without the use of pesticides and manage to do so – most of the time. But sometimes, when caterpillars are on the march against my cabbages or blackflies threaten my beans, I find that a single application of the right pesticide will prevent me from losing the fruits of my labour to pests.

Chemicals aren't all bad. The chemical pesticides that are available to gardeners today bear little relation to those that were common a few decades ago. We no longer use old-style, broad-spectrum, toxic chemicals that persist in the environment for years. They've been replaced by highly regulated, targeted products, often derived from natural sources, which break down quickly and safely after use and leave minimal residues in treated plants.

Ideally, all gardeners would like to grow their food without having to intervene with chemical controls, but it's been my experience that a single, well-timed application of pesticide can prevent a pest or disease problem from ruining a crop. I believe that chemical pesticides should be used only when it's absolutely necessary.

By choosing the right product and following the directions carefully, you can be confident that your garden and your produce will remain safe, healthy and even environmentally friendly.

JANE COURTIER

crops by how they are grown. Thus, you'll find vines such as squash in the *Vine crops* chapter and long-term crops such as rhubarb in the *Permanent plantings* chapter. Each entry will provide all you need to know to grow a crop successfully, including the correct times to plant; whether it's best to start seeds indoors, sow them directly outside or buy in young plants; tips on watering, fertilising and supporting plants; plus important information on how to harvest and store the crop.

Best of the Bunch boxes recommend tried-and-tested varieties, plus some promising newcomers. Varieties come and go, but the descriptions should give you an idea of the qualities to look for and enable you to judge if a new variety is worth a trial.

Problem solver sidebars summarise the symptoms and signs of the most common pest problems, growing disorders that affect a crop and common mistakes, and they offer quick suggestions on how to solve the problem – or how to avoid it the next time you plant the crop.

Each *Planting Guide* is a quick reference to the essential information you'll need before getting started. Watch for the thermometer icon in some entries. It alerts you to crops that are sensitive to heat exposure or chilling during their development. Where possible, the warning alerts you to temperature thresholds that may adversely affect the plants.

In general keep in mind that crops will mature faster in warmer conditions than in cool conditions, and plants may grow more slowly than usual during a drought, even if you provide supplemental water. The time of year you plant has an effect too, because plants grow more quickly during long days than short days.

FROM A COMMITTED ORGANIC GARDENER

Dear Reader,

Right from the start I decided to garden organically. I had a youthful ideal of saving the environment from chemical pollution. Learning how to garden the organic way was fascinating.

I discovered the intricacies of soil biology and the miracle of earthworms. I enjoyed turning raked-up leaves and kitchen waste into sweet-smelling compost. I planted flowers in my vegetable garden to attract beneficial insects. I learned how horticultural fleece can protect plants from adverse weather conditions, as well as from animal and insect pests. I enjoyed the adventure of trying out simple, non-commercial, organic methods: Would slugs really come to a beer-baited slug trap to drink and drown? Could encouraging the right type of wildlife into the garden reduce the amount of pest damage? (Yes, and yes.)

The beauty of tending an organic garden is that each year brings greater success as the natural systems become stronger. For example, I no longer put out slug traps because there is so little slug damage in my garden. I attribute this to healthy populations of slug predators that have grown over the years, especially ground beetles that live under the wood-chip mulch on paths at the border of my garden. I'm now into my third decade as an organic gardener and I am more committed than ever.

Fern Marshall Bradley

FERN MARSHALL BRADLEY

Is organic gardening for you?

In this book you'll find plenty of advice for gardening organically. Eating delicious, freshly picked produce, enjoying the outdoors and feeling connected with nature are the top reasons gardeners give for tending a vegetable garden. Many gardeners prefer organic methods, avoiding chemical pesticides – they love the idea that the food they are growing is pesticide-free. But what happens when things go wrong and organic solutions don't seem to work?

The two authors of this book have different answers to this question. Jane Courtier takes the view that organic methods are the first, best choice, but believes there can be a place for carefully chosen chemical pesticides if a serious insect or disease problem arises. Fern Marshall Bradley writes from the viewpoint of a longtime organic gardener who has chosen not to use chemicals in her garden. Together they've created a book that looks at vegetable gardening from both sides.

As experienced gardeners and gardening writers, Jane and Fern know that there are substantive issues on both sides to consider when deciding whether to be purely organic or not – and in the end, it's an individual choice. Let them help you make up your mind!

Part 1

YOUR GARDEN

1 Planning your garden

Planning a vegetable garden – whether in your own garden or in an allotment – can be almost as exciting as growing the vegetables, and it will ensure that your efforts bring maximum rewards. Think about the type of garden you already have and the type you want. What vegetables would be the best to grow? How can you make the best use of the space you have? What difficulties are there to overcome? The following pages will guide you through all the choices you have to make and provide some new ideas to inspire you.

Your vegetable garden can be decorative and inspiring or functional and plain – the choice is yours. Among the vegetables in this attractive garden are chard, fennel, lettuce and cabbage.

The benefits of planning

Once you have decided to grow your own vegetables, endless possibilities open up before you. Just glancing through a seed catalogue results in a list of exciting varieties you simply have to try – but hold on, the first step is to come up with a plan.

CONSIDERING AN ALLOTMENT?

If your garden is not large enough to grow as many vegetables as you would like, consider an allotment. Contact your local council for details on availability – there is often a waiting list. If you have a choice, pick a site that has an easily accessible water supply and a secure hut where you can leave your tools and equipment safely.

Quick Tip

Out of the shade

When planning your vegetables place tall plantings such as sweet corn or those grown on trellises at the north side of the plot so they don't cast shadows on lower-growing plants.

Unless you have a huge garden and almost limitless time and skills, you probably won't grow half the things you would like to. Therefore, good planning is an important part of vegetable gardening. It enables you to think sensibly about how much space and time you can devote to your garden and what type of vegetables will be most useful to you. It also avoids that embarrassment of riches, the glut – nobody wants to spend lots of effort and time growing more beans than their family and friends can eat.

Whether you are about to start a vegetable plot from scratch or plan to adapt an existing one, spend some time with a notepad and pencil before picking up a spade. Draw up a rough plan of your garden to see how the vegetables will fit in, and how much space you can afford to give them.

There are many different styles of vegetable garden, which are discussed in the following pages. You will probably find that some of them are much more suited to your needs than others. Once you have decided on your garden style, you also need to plan which vegetables you intend to grow (see pages 18–19).

Starting a new plot

Creating your own vegetable garden from scratch is a great opportunity – it means you will be able to avoid some of the common pitfalls. Here are some points to bear in mind when planning a new vegetable plot.

Convenience. If the vegetable garden is close to the house, it will be easy to dash out and pick a few herbs or dig some vegetables for dinner. It will also encourage you to visit the vegetable garden more frequently to take care of the plants. The closer it is, the more often you'll weed, water and check for pests and diseases. Firm pathways around and across the plot will prove a boon for access – and prevent feet from becoming muddy.

Climate. Vegetables will grow best if they are sheltered from strong wind. Fences, walls and hedges can create a favourable, warm, sheltered microclimate within the garden, but be careful that they don't cast too much shade. Vegetables prefer an open, sunny position. Ideally, run rows north to south within the plot to keep shading to a minimum.

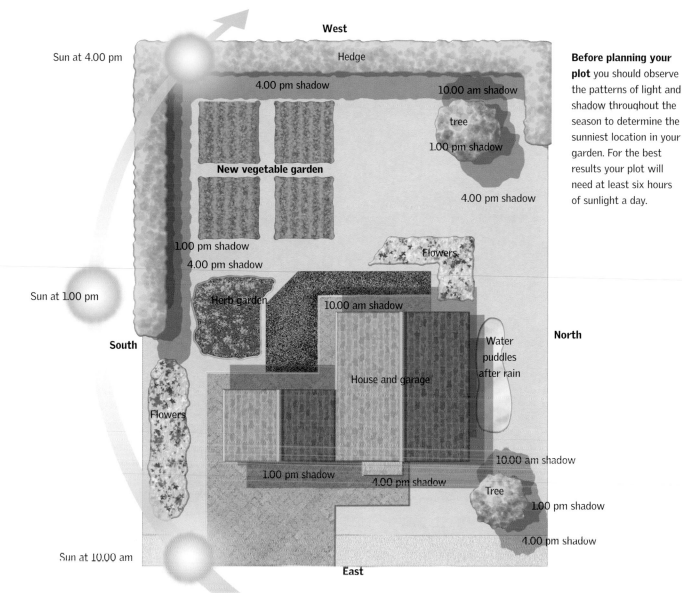

West

Sun at 4.00 pm

Hedge

4.00 pm shadow

10.00 am shadow

tree

1.00 pm shadow

New vegetable garden

4.00 pm shadow

1.00 pm shadow

4.00 pm shadow

Flowers

Sun at 1.00 pm

South

Herb garden

10.00 am shadow

North

Water puddles after rain

House and garage

Flowers

10.00 am shadow

1.00 pm shadow

4.00 pm shadow

Tree

1.00 pm shadow

4.00 pm shadow

Sun at 10.00 am

East

Before planning your plot you should observe the patterns of light and shadow throughout the season to determine the sunniest location in your garden. For the best results your plot will need at least six hours of sunlight a day.

Size. Factors that affect size include your enthusiasm, how many mouths you have to feed, how much time you have available and the size of the garden. Don't be too ambitious: a plot that is too big soon becomes a chore instead of a pleasure. As a guide a standard-sized allotment is 250sq m (300sq yd). However, most people find a half-size plot enough: that's a 9-x-13.7-m (30-x-45-ft) rectangle. Rectangles and squares are more practical than flowing shapes.

Ground preparation. What is currently on the site where you want to position your vegetable plot? Bare soil is ideal, but more likely there is a lawn, which means stripping the turf. This is not difficult if you use a sharp spade to undercut it. If it's a large area, hire a turf-cutting machine. Trees and shrubs can be difficult to remove, and a site overrun by deep-rooted perennial weeds can take taming. Consider how much time and effort you are willing to devote to this preparation.

In this typical square plot lettuce, cabbages and peas are grown in rows.

Planning your crops

By taking time to think carefully about the crops you're about to grow you can ensure that you'll get the maximum value from your vegetable garden – no matter its size.

SUCCESSIONAL PLANTING

You can have a constant supply of fresh vegetables for salads, and avoid waste from growing too much of one thing, by sowing seeds in small batches in the spring and summer.

Instead of filling one row with lettuce, another with onions and a third with radishes, sow only one row – a third of it onions, a third lettuce and a third radishes. Two weeks later, sow another row in the same way, and two weeks after that, a third row. You'll have a steady supply of the vegetables over a longer season.

Quick Tip

At the root
Never grow plants with long tap roots such as carrots and parsnips in freshly manured ground because it causes them to fork and become misshapen.

It's surprising how many times gardeners take a haphazard approach to growing vegetables. Some can't resist the lure of the seed catalogues – and before they know it, they have spent a fortune on at least twice as many packets of seeds as they have room to grow. Others fill half the plot with potatoes and cabbages every year because…well, because vegetable gardens always have potatoes and cabbages. And it's amazing how many gardeners keep on growing Brussels sprouts (or leeks, or spinach, or radishes or whatever) season after season, despite knowing that nobody in the family actually likes to eat them.

Decide what you like. Make a list of the vegetables you'd most like to grow. Unless you have endless space, concentrate on types that are difficult to buy in the shops (such as scorzonera or black salsify), are expensive (such as asparagus), benefit from being eaten freshly picked (such as corn) or are simply tastier than the commercial varieties (such as many tomatoes). Remember to ask the rest of the family for their preferences too.

Grow speciality vegetables such as artichokes to enhance your choice of vegetables for your meals.

Check the timing. Make a note of the sowing or planting times of all the crops you've listed, and when they will vacate the soil after harvesting. A spring-sown crop of broad beans, for example, will probably finish cropping by midsummer, which makes way for a quick-growing 'catch crop' such as lettuce, radishes or French beans to be sown in the same piece of ground. Make the plot work hard for its keep.

Look ahead to harvesting. Make a note of what should be cropping, month by month. Where several crops are in peak season at the same time, you should consider whether some of them can be stored successfully. It's easy to put a surplus of beans in the freezer, but it's far more difficult to cope with a glut of lettuce (see *Successional Planting*, left).

Grow for health and yield. Different vegetable crops tend to take varying quantities of nutrients from the soil. Members of the cabbage family, for example, are particularly greedy when it comes to nitrogen; conversely, peas and beans need only small amounts of soil nitrogen, because of their ability to 'fix' nitrogen from the air. Crop rotation – the practice of moving different types of vegetable crops to a different position in the garden each

By sowing little and often this gardener would have a steady supply of lettuce instead of a glut.

CROP ROTATION PLAN

The most practical rotation for most gardens is a three-year one. For the rotation to work each group must occupy the same amount of space. This makes it difficult to follow crop rotations exactly, so don't worry about achieving perfection. Keep the basic principles in mind and do the best you can. Your need to add lime depends on your soil type and pH.

	YEAR 1	YEAR 2	YEAR 3
BED 1	**Roots** Do not add manure or lime; add a balanced fertiliser in spring.	**Others** Add a balanced fertiliser in spring.	**Brassicas** Dig in manure or compost in autumn; add lime in spring.
BED 2	**Brassicas** Dig in manure or compost in autumn; add lime in spring.	**Roots** Do not add manure or lime; add a balanced fertiliser in spring.	**Others** Add a balanced fertiliser in spring.
BED 3	**Others** Add a balanced fertiliser in spring.	**Brassicas** Dig in manure or compost in autumn; add lime in spring.	**Roots** Do not add manure or lime; add a balanced fertiliser in spring.

1 Roots Potatoes, carrots, beetroot, parsnips.

3 Cabbage family Brussels sprouts, cabbage, cauliflower, plus swedes and turnips, which are also susceptible to club-root disease.

2 Others Beans, lettuce, peas, celery- and parsley-family crops, onions.

year – helps ensure that the soil does not become depleted of nutrients, which it would do if the same crops were taking the same nutrients from the same place year after year.

Different types of crops may be prone to attack by specific pests and diseases. Club-root disease, for example, attacks all members of the cabbage family (brassicas), but it has no effect on carrots, lettuces, tomatoes or other non-cabbage-family plants.

Crop rotation can help to prevent the build-up of some of these specific soil-borne pests and diseases; however, it is not 100 per cent effective. Some diseases such as club root can remain dormant in the soil for as long as 20 years, so a three- or four-year rotation plan is unlikely to starve the disease-causing organisms into submission. However, crop rotation is still effective in preventing other disease problems.

The kitchen garden

It's great to have a garden that's big enough to devote a special area to growing vegetables, as well as fruits and herbs – a traditional kitchen garden. However, large plots require careful planning to ensure they will work well without becoming too time-consuming.

IS A KITCHEN GARDEN FOR YOU?

PROS

• Hedges, fences or walls provide sheltered conditions.

• You can train fruit trees up walls and fences.

• Plenty of room for a variety of vegetables, fruits and herbs.

CONS

• Hedges, fences or walls cause problems with shade.

• Hedges will compete for water and nutrients.

• Soil between rows will become compacted; you'll need to dig the plot over at the end of the season.

• Bare soil between rows can quickly be colonised by weeds.

• The size of a large plot can be daunting, especially when it comes to such tasks as weeding.

• If the plot is large, you may sow too much of a crop.

In the past a large, traditional walled kitchen garden in the grounds of a sizeable house was regarded as useful but dull. It was hidden away at the end of the main garden and screened from view by hedges or walls.

A modern kitchen garden

Today, a kitchen garden refers to a garden with a mixture of vegetables, fruits and herbs. It can be just as decorative and interesting as any flower garden – and there's certainly no need to hide it away from view. In fact, as with any vegetable garden, it is best near the kitchen to make it easier to dig up some leeks or cut a cabbage head in cold weather.

You can provide an old-fashioned traditional touch by including walls, fences or hedges surrounding the garden, or you can leave the plot open to view. Alternatively, you can train a row of cordon or espalier apple and pear trees to make a productive dividing line between the ornamental

Trellises, pergolas and other types of support frames are ideal in the kitchen garden for growing plants that climb such as beans and peas. They also break up the space, creating outdoor garden rooms.

and kitchen areas of the garden. This will add interest by creating an extra garden 'room' without hiding the vegetables, fruits and herbs completely from view.

How does your garden grow?

Vegetables are traditionally grown in straight rows in a single, large, square or rectangular plot. There are usually gaps between the rows to allow the gardener to care for the plants.

Instead of growing vegetables in one large plot, try growing them in a bed system, thereby avoiding the drawbacks of a traditional kitchen garden (see *Is a Kitchen Garden for You?*, left).

Divide the space into a series of beds divided by pathways. Make sure the beds are narrow enough to be reached from the pathways on each side (see *Creating a Bed System,* below right). This will allow you to work in the garden without compacting the soil by treading on it. (This growing system is also used for no-dig gardens: see pages 42–43.)

Crop rows can be grown more closely together because access is not necessary, so weeds have less of a chance to gain a foothold. The bed system makes it easy to plan rotations and sow in short rows for successional planting (see pages 18–19). Smaller beds also mean work can be divided into small sections at a time.

CREATING A BED SYSTEM

Before marking out the beds, cultivate the whole plot as you would for any vegetable garden, removing all perennial weeds and raking the soil level.

Make the beds 1.2m (4ft) wide so you can reach across half the bed from each side. Because you'll have to walk to the end of the bed to reach the other side, a maximum of 3m (10ft) is a good length. Make the pathways at least 45cm (18in) wide, with a few 60- to 90-cm (2- to 3-ft)-wide pathways, which will be suitable for wheelbarrow access.

Beds can be made level with the surrounding ground, but an edging helps to define them more clearly, and a raised edging allows you to build the beds up by adding organic matter (see pages 22–23).

Surface the pathways in a vegetable garden with bark chips or gravel, preferably on top of a landscape fabric (these are available from garden centres), which will help suppress weed growth.

Raised beds

Raised beds may be low – just a few centimetres above the surrounding ground level – or about waist height, which is especially useful for gardeners with mobility problems.

Many people who grow their vegetables in raised beds follow the no-dig method of cultivation (see pages 42–43). Because no-dig gardeners add large amounts of compost and other organic matter to their beds, the surface of the beds soon becomes higher than the surrounding soil. Although the soil and organic matter can simply be mounded up with sloping sides, using edging to contain the soil is more practical, especially as the layers build up over a few years.

Low beds

The height of a low bed can vary from 10–30cm (4–12in) high, and it may be made from a range of materials, including wood, bricks, blocks and edging tiles. Wood is perhaps the most commonly used

material, but it should be treated with a safe wood preservative to ensure a reasonably long life.

Old railway sleepers were once commonly used to make raised beds, but because they were treated with creosote, these are unsuitable for garden use. (However, safe, untreated sleepers are sometimes available.) Garden centres and builders' suppliers stock decorative edging materials.

You can stack a few layers of bricks or use them on end for extra height. Don't slope them on an angle – the corners could scrape your knees as you do your gardening.

MAKING A LOW BED

You can make a suitable edging from wood planks that are 2.5cm (1in) thick and 15cm (6in) wide. For rigidity sink the planks 5cm (2in) deep into the ground and support them with 2.5-cm (1-in)-square pegs every 1.2m (4ft); nail them to similar pegs that will serve as corner posts.

Alternatively, you can set concrete blocks or bricks into a shallow trench, which will provide stability to these edgings. Make sure you pack the soil tightly around them to hold them in place.

DIMENSIONS FOR RAISED BEDS

	Height	Width (one-sided access)	Width (two-sided access)
Wheelchair gardener	60–75cm (24–30in)	60cm (24in)	90–120cm (36–48in)
Standing gardener	75–90cm (30–36in)	60cm (24in)	120cm (48in)

These can range from inexpensive rolls of plastic to extravagant, beautiful and sometimes expensive antique-style tiles.

High beds

In situations where growing in the ground is impossible – a garden with a solid surface, for example, or where the soil is polluted – high raised beds are ideal. They are also good for gardeners who find bending difficult or impossible, who are wheelchair users or who suffer the annoyances of increasing age such as worsening eyesight, stiffening joints and tiring easily. Raised beds can also be a design statement, adding three-dimensional interest to the garden scene.

If you want to build a raised bed simply for its decorative appeal, you can make it whatever height you like. However, if it is to make gardening easier, the height and width of the bed will depend on who is going to use it, particularly whether it is a gardener who needs to work from a seated position or a wheelchair (see *Dimensions for Raised Beds*, left), or someone who will work standing up.

Gardeners who use a wheelchair will find it much easier to work at a bed designed like a table, where there will be room to roll the wheelchair underneath. Otherwise access will be limited and awkward, involving twisting and stretching. Detailed dimensions and advice are available from many disability groups.

Quick Tip

A super-sized pot

Like pots and containers, raised beds dry out more quickly than the open ground and need frequent watering. Without the proper drainage materials and holes, they can also become waterlogged in wet weather.

CONSTRUCTING A TALL RAISED BED

Tall raised beds are often built from wood, but you can also build them from bricks or stone. If you plan to build the raised bed on soil start with a concrete footing to provide a firm, level surface.

The walls will need to be only one brick thick. To allow for drainage, leave some weep holes at the base of the walls. Finish the walls with suitable coping stones for weather protection; if you choose wide, flat coping it can also double as garden seating.

A mixture of peas and lettuces thrives in this raised bed, which also serves as a frame for nasturtiums.

Because plants grow only in the top 30cm (12in) or so, fill the base with rubble, which will also improve drainage. Finish off with 45cm (18in) of good-quality topsoil, so that it is level with or slightly mounded above the walls to allow for settling.

Wood, metal and other materials are often used for sidings, too.

Ornamental vegetable gardens

Many vegetables are beautiful – a feast for the eyes as well as the palate. Many varieties are worth growing for their decorative value, whether it's in a carefully planned formal plot known as a potager or mingled with flowers in an ornamental border.

GUIDELINES FOR A FORMAL POTAGER

• Keep the design simple so that weeding and general care of the plants are made easier.

• If you want an edging plant, choose one that doesn't need clipping (such as curly-leaved parsley or golden pot marigolds).

• Choose vegetables that you can sample without spoiling their decorative effect. French and climbing beans, peppers and asparagus peas, for example, can all be picked freely, while taking a few carefully chosen leaves from cut-and-come-again lettuce, kale and Swiss chard won't do any harm.

• Plant late-maturing varieties of vegetables such as leeks, onions, cabbages, carrots and cauliflower to avoid making a hole in the display.

Originally, the French term '*potager*' referred to a kitchen garden that supplied vegetables for the soup pot. However, today it has come to mean a formal vegetable plot where the plants are grown for their ornamental potential, as well as for their crops.

The potager usually consists of a number of beds that are arranged in a neat, geometric pattern – rectangles, squares, diamonds, triangles or circles. The beds are often edged with dwarf hedges, traditionally of box, and are filled with vegetables carefully chosen for their shapes, colours and textures.

While a small-scale potager for the home garden can look splendid, don't underestimate the amount of work involved. A formal potager must be kept neat if it is to look attractive, and that means frequent weeding and careful attention to pest and disease control.

Dwarf hedges look lovely, but remember that they will need lots of clipping (and that 'dwarf' usually means crawling along on your hands and knees with the secateurs). In addition, unless you're prepared to ruin your carefully planned display, you won't be able to harvest many of the vegetables.

The large cabbage leaves make an impact planted next to flowers in this garden.

Vegetables in flower borders

An easier way to grow vegetables for their decorative qualities is to mix them with flowers and shrubs in an ornamental border. Use plants such as climbing beans on a tepee of canes or stately globe artichokes to provide tall focal points at the back of the border, and fill the front of the beds with low-growing edgers such as frilly-leaved lettuce or parsley, or culinary thyme.

Groups of bold, textured Swiss chard, colourful bush tomatoes, hummocks of French beans and lacy-leaved carrots can fill in the middle ground alongside flowering perennials or shrubs.

The dark red leaves of chard are the perfect foil for these bright cosmos.

Quick Tip

New favourites

When growing vegetables for their decorative qualities, you should always check the latest seed catalogues. New, ornamental varieties of old favourites are introduced every year, reflecting their growing popularity.

ORNAMENTAL VEGETABLES

Here are just a few suggestions for vegetables that have decorative qualities. These will look stunning in most flower borders. You can also try experimenting with other vegetable varieties, including bush tomatoes.

Artichokes With their tall, stately habit and architectural, jagged-edged, silver leaves, globe artichokes make a bold and brilliant statement in any garden.

Asparagus peas An open-growing bush with attractive trifoliate leaves and lovely cinnamon-red, pealike flowers. These are followed by unusual and delicious winged pods.

Bean (runner) These have a climbing habit with attractive, scarlet flowers all summer. 'Hestia' is an unusual non-climbing dwarf variety that has red and white flowers.

Peppers Small-fruited chilli peppers are eye-catching; try 'Etna', with brilliant red fruits in upright clusters, or 'Fiesta' with yellow, purple or red peppers.

Herbs Try varieties in unusual colours such as purple-leaved or variegated sage, purple basil, golden thyme and golden marjoram. Fennel has a delicate ferny foliage, and the bronze variety is particularly striking.

Swiss chard 'Bright Lights' is one of the best mixtures, with red, gold, pink, white, orange and violet stems topped with deeply quilted, rich green leaf blades.

Lettuce Any good seed catalogue will feature many handsome lettuces: 'Lollo Rossa' and 'Lollo Bionda' are old favourites with crisply crimped, frilly leaves, and

there are some excellent oak-leaved types such as deep red 'Flamenco' or 'Delicata'.

Salad onion Try red-shanked 'Rossa Lunga de Firenze' or 'North Holland Blood Red'.

Summer squash There is no end of varieties here: 'Sunburst' and 'Nova' both have golden, scalloped patty-pan fruits; 'Nova' also has contrasting green tips. Slender, bottle-shaped 'Zephyr' has yellow fruits that look as though the tips have been dipped into pale green paint.

The interesting fruits and large architectural leaves of squash make an unusual, attractive addition to an ornamental garden.

Vegetables in small spaces

No garden is too small to grow a few vegetables – you can grow reasonably sized crops in the smallest of spaces, even on balconies and patios.

Few gardeners are lucky enough to have a huge garden with limitless space for vegetables. Even in large gardens, vegetables often compete for space with decorative flowers and shrubs. Modern gardens are becoming smaller and smaller, and in some cases only a tiny patio garden or compact balcony is available.

With such limitations, it is easy to think that home-grown vegetables are out of the question – however, that's not the case. First of all, vegetables and flowers can co-exist happily in an ornamental garden (see pages 24–25), and if soil beds are not available many vegetables grow well in containers (see pages 44–45), which are ideal for patios and balconies. Even a kitchen window sill can be pressed into use for growing herbs and perhaps a chilli pepper or a compact variety of tomato.

What to grow

The choice of vegetables is important where space is limited. Consider the following points when choosing them:

Colourful red and yellow peppers brighten up a small patio vegetable garden.

High yielding. A container that has been planted with one courgette will supply you with up to 15 fruits over the summer – enough for several meals. However, the same container planted with spinach might give you enough leaves for only a single serving – if you are lucky. When choosing plants, look for ones that give the maximum return for the space they occupy. Good choices include climbing beans, tomatoes, courgettes and lettuce.

High value. Main-crop potatoes are easy to find and inexpensive when bought from the shops, so don't consider growing them if you're short of space. However, early or out-of-season potatoes are a different matter; get the timing right and you could be enjoying home-grown new potatoes at a time when they cost a fortune at the shops – or when they are completely unobtainable. Likewise, instead of growing common lettuce, seek out seeds of frilly-leaved or coloured varieties that fetch a premium in the shops; grow red salad onions instead of the normal white ones or globe-rooted carrots instead of the usual long varieties.

Easy to grow. The smaller the space for growing, the smaller your margin for error. If one lettuce in a row of 20 bolts to seed, it's not a disaster; however, if it's one lettuce out of only three, it assumes much greater significance. Of course, your success rate will depend on your garden conditions and your experience, and these will affect your choices.

Vegetables and herbs such as asparagus, cabbage, sage, thyme and marjoram can be added to a flower border.

In this hanging basket French marigolds add a splash of colour, while sage and lettuce provide a leafy backdrop.

CHOOSING THE VEGETABLES

GOOD TO GROW

• **Lettuce** Choose cut-and-come-again varieties to provide a steady supply of leaves; also select varieties that are difficult to find or expensive to buy.

• **Green beans** Look for dwarf varieties that can be grown in a hanging basket; you can also grow climbing varieties in containers.

• **Tomatoes** Look for varieties specially bred for trailing over a hanging basket such as 'Balconi' or 'Gartenperle'.

• **Courgette** Golden-fruited types such as 'Gold Rush' provide a bright splash of colour in a container.

AVOID

• **Cauliflower** It is prone to several pests and diseases and will not form good heads unless the soil conditions are perfect.

• **Globe artichokes** These large plants take up lots of space, yet they only provide a small yield.

• **Chicory** It needs forcing and careful blanching.

• **Spinach** It shoots to seed quickly in warm, dry weather and needs lots of space for a reasonable crop.

• **Cucumber** (Greenhouse types) Do not allow the flowers to be fertilised, or bitter and misshapen fruits may result.

Problem gardens

Not every garden is perfect for growing vegetables – however, there are often simple solutions for most common problems. You can enjoy growing your own produce in even the most unpromising situations.

VEGETABLES FOR A PARTIALLY SHADY PLOT

On a partially shady plot, there's little point in growing sun-loving vegetables such as tomatoes and peppers. However, if your plot receives a minimum of two to three hours of sun a day, you can successfully grow the following moderately shade-tolerant vegetables and herbs:

beetroot	kohlrabi	rhubarb
broccoli	lettuce	salsify
chives	mint	spinach
garlic	parsley	turnips
kale	radishes	

Quick Tip

Whitewash

Shade cast by buildings can be difficult to handle, but you can maximise the amount of available light by painting all the surrounding surfaces white.

Most vegetables need plenty of direct sunlight to grow and crop well: six hours of summer sun each day is considered ideal. Good light will encourage sturdy growth and good leaf formation, which will enable the plant to carry out efficient food production through photosynthesis. This, in turn, will lead to heavier and better-quality crops.

Shady situations

Excessive shade will result in spindly plants that are more vulnerable to pest and disease attack. They often fail to reach their full cropping potential.

If the shade is cast by tree and shrub branches, this is usually easy to deal with by pruning or removing the plants involved. (However, if the problem plants are on a neighbour's property, preserve good relations by first discussing your pruning plans with your neighbour.) Consider lowering tall hedges to reduce the amount of shadow they cast – you will still retain the benefit of their protection. Walls and fences also offer valuable protection for vegetables, but they can cast a deep shadow if they are too tall. Consider replacing part of the wall or fence with a lower barrier on the side that causes the most shade problems.

Temperature extremes

Vegetables are either warm-season lovers or cool-season types. Warm-season crops are sensitive to any frost and need a long, hot growing season to do well. Temperatures must be above 15.5°C (60°F) – a temperature of 21°C (70°F) is preferable. Cool-season vegetables that are moderately hardy to frost hardy will do best in growing temperatures of 15.5–26.5°C (60–80°F). Sustained periods of higher temperatures will reduce both yields and crop quality.

In most temperate regions both warm-season and cool-season crops can be grown successfully as long as the timing is right. In cool areas use cloches and horticultural fleece to provide extra protection from low temperatures, and start plants indoors to gain an early start to the growing season (see pages 74–81).

Low-lying areas of the garden may become frost pockets. Because cool air sinks, it rolls down to the base of a hill and settles there in a chilly pool.

Terracing will create flat beds for growing vegetables. The walls help support the soil.

A solid barrier such as a wall or fence can cause a frost pocket to form by preventing the cold air from flowing down the hill, so bear this in mind when putting up barriers around the vegetable garden.

In hot climates time the sowing of cool-season vegetables so that they crop in spring or autumn, and avoid the hottest months. Provide shade and overhead irrigation to lower temperatures and avoid drought stress.

Slopes

A gently sloping garden is not too much of a problem for vegetable growing, particularly if you are lucky enough for the slope to face the right direction and allow the plants to bask in extra sunshine. However, a steep slope can be a real problem, and it can easily provide you with a demonstration of how soil erosion occurs – it takes little time for rain to wash soil down to the base of the slope. In this situation terracing is the only answer. Use the 'cut and fill' method by cutting partially into the slope and partially building it out to make one or more flat beds for growing vegetables.

Soil problems

The majority of poor soils can be improved (see pages 32–39). However, if your garden soil is unsuitable for vegetable growing – it is shallow or stony or it has been polluted by industrial waste – you can grow vegetables in containers or raised beds filled with imported, good-quality topsoil. If the natural soil is polluted, line the base of a raised bed with a landscaping (geotextile) fabric that will prevent the vegetables' roots from penetrating into the polluted area.

Poor drainage is another problem. You can improve heavy clay soil that does not drain freely by applying organic matter, but some sites have a more serious problem where water simply cannot get away because of the underlying ground structure. In this case it may be necessary to install a drainage system consisting of plastic perforated pipes or tile drains.

Wind

In exposed windy areas protect vegetable plots by erecting windbreaks. Avoid putting up a solid barrier such as a wall or close-boarded fence – this deflects the wind over the top only for it to be pulled down and cause turbulence just beyond the barrier. Windbreaks should be around 50 per cent permeable to be effective. Hedges, open-style fences or plastic windbreak netting are all good solutions for reducing the strength of the gusts to less damaging levels as they pass through them.

Raised beds and containers are a solution for gardens with poor soil conditions.

> ### VEGETABLES FOR THE RIGHT SEASON
>
> **Cool-season vegetables:**
> beetroot, broccoli, broad beans, Brussels sprouts, chives, cabbage, carrot, cauliflower, celeriac, celery, chicory, Chinese cabbage, cress, endive, fennel, garlic, kale, kohlrabi, leeks, lettuce, onions, parsley, parsnips, peas, potatoes, radicchio, radishes, rocket, salad onions, salsify, shallots, spinach, swedes, Swiss chard, turnips.
>
> **Warm-season vegetables:**
> aubergines, beans, cucumbers, melons, okra, peas, peppers, sweet potatoes, courgettes and squash, sweet corn, tomatoes.

2 Preparing the ground

Before you start sowing seeds, buying plants, and getting your vegetable garden under way, you need to ensure that the soil – the plants' home – is in good condition. For your vegetables to thrive, they need a well-prepared plot that will provide them with all the necessary food, water and support from the beginning.

Understanding how soil provides for plants will enable you to decide what you need to do: whether or not you need to dig; what you can add to your soil to improve it; and whether it needs lime or additional fertilizers. Get these right, and you'll have a successful harvest.

A well-prepared vegetable plot will provide ample rewards at harvest time.

All about soil

Soil is a wonderful material. It takes thousands of years to form – broken down from rocks by wind, rain and frost – and it is teeming with life we cannot see. Understanding soil and knowing how to look after it are vital for the production of strong, healthy plants.

Plants miraculously make food out of light and air, but to make that miracle happen, they have a few requirements. They need water and a variety of mineral nutrients, and they usually need somewhere to anchor themselves while they grow. For most plants, this is where soil comes in.

Soil may have started its life as rock, but in the process of its breakdown into tiny particles, it has acquired a few other constituents. Variations in the proportions of these constituents mean there are different types of soil, some of which are better for plant growth than others.

Before testing soil, mix it with water and shake it up. The sediment will settle in layers, and you can determine the proportions of silt, clay and organic matter in the soil.

VEGETABLE PH PREFERENCES

Most vegetables prefer soil between pH 6.5 and 7.0, but the following types will tolerate soil with higher levels of acid (below 6.0) or alkaline (above 7.0).

Acid-tolerant plants (below pH 6.0)	Alkaline-tolerant plants (above pH 7.0)	Alkaline and acid-tolerant plants
Aubergine 5.5–6.8	Asparagus 6.5–7.5	Celery
Carrot 5.5–6.8	Beetroot 6.5–7.5	Garlic
Celery 5.5–7.5	Brussels sprouts 6.0–7.5	
Endive 5.5–7.0	Cauliflower 6.0–7.5	
Garlic 5.5–7.5	Celery 5.5–7.5	
Potato 5.8–6.5	Cucumber 6.0–7.5	
Radish 5.5–6.5	Garlic 5.5–7.5	
Rhubarb 5.0–6.8	Leek 6.0–7.5	
Sweet potato 5.5–6.5	Melon 6.0–7.5	
Watermelon 5.5–7.0	Okra 6.8–7.5	
	Onion 6.0–7.5	
	Shallot 6.5–7.5	

The main constituents are:

Soil particles. The size of broken-down rock particles in soil varies: the largest are sand; smaller particles are silt; and the smallest are clay. Most soil has a mixture of sand, silt and clay. An even mixture is a loam, but one type often predominates. The soil is then known as a sandy loam, a clay loam and so on,

Organic matter. This is any living thing that has died. Plants grow in the soil, die, rot down and are absorbed back into the soil as humus. Plants are also eaten by grazing animals, who return them to the soil as manure; the animals also die and are broken down and incorporated into the soil, too.

Living organisms. In addition to the larger soil-dwelling creatures that we can easily see such as earthworms and insects, soil is full of microscopic life forms. These micro-organisms are various fungi and bacteria – many of which have an important role in breaking down plant and animal matter into humus. Not all of the soil's living population are helpful; many insects, eelworms and mites are plant pests, and some types of fungi and bacteria cause devastating diseases.

Air and water. These are essential constituents of soil. The fragile root hairs that grow from a plant's roots seek out the moisture and dissolved minerals that are vital for growth. They also need air to function, as do soil micro-organisms. The amounts of water and air within the soil depends upon its structure (see pages 34–35).

Nutrients

While plants make their own food using energy from sunlight, they need mineral nutrients to do so. When dissolved in soil moisture, these nutrients are taken up by the roots.

The major nutrients required are nitrogen, phosphorus and potassium – often abbreviated to their chemical symbols of N, P and K. Nitrogen helps leafy growth, phosphorus helps provide root development and potassium encourages flowers and fruits.

Other mineral nutrients needed in smaller quantities are calcium, sulphur and magnesium, plus trace elements, which include iron, boron, copper, manganese, molybdenum and zinc.

SOIL ACIDITY

Soil may be acid, alkaline or neutral. Most vegetables grow best in soil that is just on the acid side of neutral. However, if the soil becomes too acid, club-root disease, which affects members of the cabbage family, can become a real problem. Conversely, soil that is too alkaline can 'lock up' various nutrients and make them unavailable to plants.

Soil acidity is measured on a pH scale: a pH between 1.0 and 7.0 is acid; pH 7.0 to 14.0 is alkaline and pH 7.0 is neutral. Simple soil-testing kits, available from garden centres, reveal your soil's acidity, but do several tests in different parts of the garden for the best results. For a more detailed analysis, you can send samples to a commerical laboratory for testing.

Most vegetables grow best at about pH 6.5. If the soil is more acid than this apply ground limestone to reduce the acidity.

this is especially helpful to prevent club root in cabbage-family plants. Depending on the soil, the amount of lime to apply varies. As a guide, add: 270g to sandy soil, 540g to a mixed loam and 800g to clay per sq m (or ½lb, 1lb or 1½lb per sq yd). This raises the pH by one unit – for example, from pH 5.5 to pH 6.5.

Lowering the pH of an alkaline soil is not practical, but knowing your soil is alkaline will warn you that you may need to apply a fertiliser that contains trace elements.

Dip a test strip into soil mixed with water and compare its colour with those on the chart.

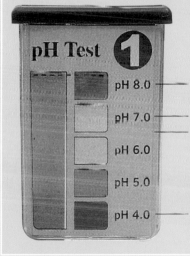

pH Test **1**

pH 8.0 —— pH 7.0 to 14.0 is alkaline

pH 7.0 —— pH 7.0 is neutral
—— pH 6.5 is best for most vegetables

pH 6.0

pH 5.0

pH 4.0 —— pH 1.0 to 7.0 is acid

Different soils vary in the quantity and quality of these nutrients. If sufficient nutrients are not present in the soil, they can be added in the form of manure, compost or various manufactured fertilisers. Soil-test kits for checking your soil's nutrient status are available from garden centres.

Quick Tip

Telltale blooms

If you have a bigleaf hydrangea (*Hydrangea macrophylla*), you can use the colour of its blooms to determine the soil pH where it is planted: pink, above pH 7.0; blue, pH 6.5 or lower; both pink and blue, neutral at pH 7.0.

Improving your soil

Few gardens are blessed with perfect soil, but fortunately there's plenty that can be done to improve it. Building up soil fertility will pay dividends in heavier, tastier crops.

Imagine a glass jar filled with golf balls. Because the balls are relatively big, there are large air spaces between them. Now imagine the same jar filled with dried peas – the air spaces between the peas are much smaller. If the jar is filled with sugar crystals the spaces between the crystals are comparatively minute.

This is a little like soil. Sandy soil has large particles with plenty of air surrounding them. Soil that is mainly silt has smaller air spaces and slow water drainage, while clay particles have tiny air spaces between them, and water is often trapped by surface tension around the particles.

Identifying your soil

The best garden soil is loam, made up of a mixture of sand, silt and clay. Moisten a pinch of soil and rub it between your thumb and forefinger. Sandy soil feels gritty, silty soil feels slippery and clay soil feels sticky. Try moulding a handful of moist soil into a ball. If it falls apart it's sandy; if it moulds easily into a ball it contains lots of clay. If you can give the ball of soil a polish with your thumb, there's an even higher proportion of clay.

Sandy soil has large particles and drains rapidly. It dries quickly in hot weather.

Loam consists of a friable (crumbly) mixture of sand, silt and clay.

To do a clay test squeeze a ball of moist soil in your hand. If it forms a firm ball it's clay.

Clay soil has tiny particles that trap water and can make the soil waterlogged.

Sandy soil is quick to warm up in spring, is light and easy to manage and is rarely waterlogged. However, it is a hungry, thirsty soil, because water and dissolved nutrients drain through it before plants can use them.

A heavy, clay soil remains cold for longer in spring, and it is difficult to dig. It soon becomes waterlogged and airless in wet weather, yet it can bake rock hard in droughts. However, clay soil usually contains good quantities of vital plant nutrients.

Improving soil structure

The structure of both very heavy and very light soil can be greatly improved by adding organic matter.

Fibrous organic matter helps to break up clay soil, making it easier to dig, and it encourages soil particles to stick together so that drainage is improved. In free-draining soils it acts like a sponge, soaking up moisture and holding onto it so that it remains available to plants. (For more about organic matter see pages 36–39.)

Cultivation

Digging and forking are cultivation techniques that involve turning over and mixing layers of soil. This helps to break up the hard surface soil cap to let in air and moisture. It allows heavy, sticky soil to be broken down by exposing it to the weather, it incorporates organic matter and it breaks up any hard layers of soil that have formed below the surface.

However, cultivation does have its drawbacks. Carelessly done, it can damage soil structure and cause compaction on heavy soils; it can also bring buried weed seeds up to the surface where they can germinate.

Quick Tip

Walking a plank

Clay soil is easily compacted when wet. Avoid walking on wet clay soil and taking heavy equipment such as wheelbarrows across it. Where you cannot avoid it, put a plank down to walk or push a wheelbarrow on – it will help to spread the load and limit the damage.

EARTHWORMS

The presence of earthworms will greatly improve the structure of your soil. They make burrows, which help to bring air into the soil and allow water to drain away. These burrows may extend as far as 2m (6ft) below the surface of the soil.

Earthworms eat organic matter such as dead leaves, rising up to the surface and dragging the leaves down into their burrows. They also ingest soil as they burrow through it, depositing the sifted remains as casts either on the soil surface or within the burrow. These habits incorporate large amounts of surface organic matter into the soil and begin the process of breaking it down. They also mix up the layers of soil.

Earthworms can be encouraged by spreading large amounts of organic matter such as compost and leaf mould (see pages 36–37) on the soil surface. They are usually particularly abundant in no-dig plots (see pages 42–43) because of the amount of organic matter used. In fact, they will do the soil mixing and 'digging' for you.

Worms sold as bait in fishing shops are brandling worms. Don't be tempted to buy these worms to add to garden soil; they don't do the same job as earthworms.

CULTIVATING YOUR SOIL

You will find these tools essential for soil cultivation.

Tool	Use
Spade	For digging: keep the blade clean and sharp so that it slices down into the soil with minimum effort. Stainless steel spades are easier to use because the soil doesn't stick to them. However, they are more expensive to buy.
Fork	Good for easing out perennial weeds without breaking their roots and for lifting mature vegetables.
Rake	Breaks the soil surface down into really fine crumbs and levels it for sowing seeds and planting; also removes surface stones and weed debris.
Trowel	For digging individual planting holes or removing deep-rooted weeds.

Enriching your soil

Organic matter is a valuable addition to almost any soil; however, you'll need a lot of it for even an average-sized vegetable garden. A compost heap is one way to obtain organic matter – for free – but there are other ways of obtaining useful organic matter too.

OTHER SOURCES OF ORGANIC MATTER

Depending on where you live, you may be able to obtain other useful organic products.

• Mushroom compost is rotted horse manure previously used for growing a crop of mushrooms. Lime is used in the mushroom-growing process, so it is not suitable for alkaline, chalky soils.

• Spent hops are available cheaply or free from breweries. They are difficult to handle because they are wet, and they will give your garden a distinctly interesting aroma when fresh.

• If you live near the coast you can collect seaweed, which is rich in nutrients. It is wet and bulky, and it can attract flies unless covered, so add it to the compost heap in small quantities.

By its nature, organic matter is bulky, often making it difficult to transport. However, if you can overcome that problem, there are useful sources that can be valuable for improving your garden soil.

Compost. Home-made compost is the primary source of organic matter for most gardens. It helps dispose of waste plant material, and it is on site, ready to use. (For making compost see pages 38–39.)

Leaf mould. Because they take longer to break down, you should compost autumn leaves on their own instead of adding them to the compost heap. You can make a standard compost heap for them (see page 39), but a simple way to compost leaves is to place them in plastic sacks along with a few layers of garden soil. Tie the neck of the sack when it is full, puncture the sides of the bag several times with a garden fork to provide air holes, then leave the bags in an out-of-the-way corner for six months to a year until the mixture is dark brown and crumbly.

Autumn leaves are composted in a separate pile on their own and will eventually turn into leaf mould.

Manure. Animal manures are excellent soil additives, providing useful quantities of plant nutrients as well as having a beneficial effect on soil structure. Allow manure to rot down before you use it in the garden. Fresh manure can scorch plant roots if it comes into contact with them. It also uses nitrogen as it starts to decompose and will take that nitrogen from the soil, stealing it from the plants. Stack manure into a pile and allow it to rot down, or add it to the garden compost heap.

Horse manure is probably one of the most available types, and it tends to rot down more quickly than farmyard manures from cows and pigs.

Poultry manure is lightweight but caustic and will need to be well rotted before you can use it, so add it to the compost heap. It can be extremely smelly, and because it may come from animals raised in crowded, unethical conditions, you may also have moral objections to using it.

Manures are often mixed with the animals' bedding. Straw is much better than wood shavings, which will take a long time to decompose.

Using organic matter

It is usually best to compost organic matter before using it. However, you can use fresh organic matter by spreading it on a cleared vegetable plot in the autumn, because it will have time to rot down before sowing and planting in the spring.

You can add organic matter to the soil in three ways: place it in the base of a trench and cover with soil; mix it into the soil with a fork or spade; or apply it as a surface layer (called a mulch), which will be taken down into the soil gradually by earthworms. Placing it in the bottom of a trench is a good method for thirsty plants with deep roots such as scarlet runner

Green manure plants have been chopped down and left to wilt. They will be dug into the soil where they will add nutrients, which will enrich it.

beans, where it will form a spongy moisture reservoir. Mix the organic matter with the soil if you want to get it to the area quickly where plants can take advantage of it. If you spread organic matter as a mulch, earthworms will do the same job but they take more time. Mulching also suppresses weed growth, retains soil moisture (if the soil is already moist) and prevents an impenetrable crust or cap from forming on the soil surface.

Green manure

Plants that are grown specifically to be dug into the soil are known as green manure. They are useful as a cover crop where an area of the vegetable plot is left bare for several weeks, because they help prevent weeds from taking over and, when dug in, they enrich the soil for the next crop.

Sow green manures in late summer and early autumn and cut them down in spring; or sow in early spring and cut down as the space is needed. Dig the plants in while they are young, before they flower, to prevent the plants from self-seeding and spreading new plants.

PLANTS FOR GREEN MANURE

Here are the most popular plants for green manures:

- Pulses (members of the pea and bean family) because they have the unique ability to take nitrogen from the air and convert it into a form that is usable to plants (this is known as nitrogen fixing).

- Alfalfa (lucerne), clover, agricultural lupin, vetch and other nitrogen-fixing plants. Others such as buckwheat, rye, oats, millet and mustard

Quick Tip

Buying manure

Because most animal manures are so bulky, several proprietary, pre-rotted, bagged manures are available from garden centres. They are more expensive but easier to transport.

3 Sowing and planting

The really exciting part of vegetable growing is witnessing the conversion of a packet of dry, shrivelled-looking seeds into rows of vigorous, healthy plants. It is important to remember that vegetable plants are at their most vulnerable stage when they are young and need special care. The following pages contain advice to help you give your seedlings and young plants the best possible start, whether you are sowing them directly in the vegetable plot or in containers for transplanting – or if you are bypassing the sowing stage altogether and buying young plants.

Some young plants will benefit from a protective cover, whether provided by cloches, a cold frame or a greenhouse.

A planting strategy

Careful planning is the best way to get the most from your vegetable garden. Many gardeners don't have the space – or time – to grow everything they would like, so it's a matter of establishing your priorities before you start buying tempting packets of seeds!

The following questions will help you get a better idea of your requirements and limitations so that you can plan your crops effectively:

What do you want from your vegetable garden? You should think about the reasons you want to grow vegetables. You may be determined to grow all the vegetables necessary to supply your household needs so you can be sure of enjoying fresh, healthy, organically grown produce at all times. Or perhaps it's the fun and challenge of actually growing the crops that appeal to you most – and the harvest is a welcome bonus. Some gardeners are content to continue buying reasonably inexpensive staples such as potatoes at the shops and concentrate on growing the more unusual and exotic vegetables that are expensive or difficult to find.

How much space do you have? This is a limiting factor for many gardeners. If you want to get the most out of a small area concentrate on the crops that produce the biggest potential harvest per m (ft) of row. In the *Guide to Vegetable Yields* (left), these weights are only approximate. The actual yields vary considerably, according to your soil type, climate and expertise. However, the chart will enable you to compare the different crops. If space is limited, for example, runner

GUIDE TO VEGETABLE YIELDS

The following yields are for planting a row 1m (3ft) long.

Vegetable	Yield	Vegetable	Yield
Bean, runner	6kg (13lb)	Salad onion	340g (12oz)
Bean, French	1.5kg (3lb)	Squash	4kg (9lb)
Beetroot	2.5kg (5lb)	Spinach	1kg (2lb)
Broccoli, sprouting	1kg (2lb)	Swede	2kg (4½lb)
Brussels sprout	2kg (4½lb)	Sweet corn	2lb (1kg)
Cabbage	3.2kg (7lb)	Tomato	7lb (3.2kg)
Carrot	3.2kg (7lb)	Turnip	2kg (4½lb)
Cauliflower	2kg (4½lb)		
Celery	1.5kg (3lb)		
Chinese cabbage	1.5kg (3lb)		
Courgette	3kg (6½lb)		
Leek	3.2kg (7lb)		
Lettuce	1kg (2lb)		
Onion, bulb	2.5kg (5lb)		
Parsnip	3.2kg (7lb)		
Pea	2kg (4½lb)		
Potato	4kg (9lb)		

Runner beans will produce a much greater yield than dwarf beans.

beans will be a better option in your garden than spinach.

It's also useful to know how long a crop will occupy the ground (see *Sowing to Harvest Times,* below); you can grow a whole series of short-term crops such as lettuce and radishes in the time it takes Brussels sprouts or winter cabbage to mature.

How much time do you have? If you are trying to grow vegetables as part of a busy working and family life, you probably won't have as much time for growing vegetables as someone with plenty of time on his or her hands, who sees vegetable gardening as a serious hobby. You should be sensible about the hours you can put in and choose crops that are easy to care for, instead of labour-intensive ones if you have little time on your hands.

Be realistic about your capabilities. If you are new to vegetable growing, you can build your confidence with easy crops such as lettuce, carrots and beans before trying the challenge of aubergines or cauliflower.

What about the family? Consider how many people you are growing for – there's no point in producing dozens of courgettes, tomatoes or lettuce if there are just two of you to eat them. And don't forget people's likes and dislikes, too. It is surprising how many gardeners grow Brussels sprouts or parsnips, although no one in the family enjoys them.

SOWING TO HARVEST TIMES

The chart below provides the average length of time you will need to wait between sowing seeds and harvesting your vegetables.

Short-term crop	Time	Medium-term crop	Time	Long-term crop	Time
Asparagus pea	8 to 10 weeks	Aubergine	20 weeks	Artichoke, globe	8 months
Bean, French	8 to 12 weeks	Bean, broad	14 to 26 weeks	Artichoke, Jerusalem	40 to 50 weeks
Bean, runner	12 to 14 weeks	Carrot	16 to 20 weeks	Asparagus	12 months
Beetroot	12 to 16 weeks	Cabbage (summer		Broccoli, sprouting	40 weeks
Broccoli	12 to 16 weeks	and autumn)	20 to 26 weeks	Brussels sprout	28 to 36 weeks
Cabbage, Chinese		Cauliflower		Cabbage (spring)	30 to 36 weeks
(and Asian greens)	10 to 14 weeks	(summer)	20 to 26 weeks	Cauliflower (spring)	40 to 46 weeks
Carrot (early)	12 to 16 weeks	Celery	18 to 30 weeks	Celeriac	30 to 35 weeks
Corn salad	16 weeks	Herbs	12 to 18 weeks	Garlic	24 to 30 weeks
Courgette and		Pea	12 to 32 weeks	Horseradish	28 to 30 weeks
marrow	10 to 14 weeks	Peppers	18 weeks	Kale	30 to 35 weeks
Cucumber	12 to 14 weeks	Potato	20 to 22 weeks	Leek	30 to 45 weeks
Fennel	10 to 14 weeks	Potato, sweet	18 to 24 weeks	Onion, bulb	22 to 46 weeks
Kohlrabi	8 to 12 weeks	Pumpkin and		Parsnip	34 weeks
Lettuce	6 to 14 weeks	winter squash	10 to 19 weeks	Rhubarb	15 months
Mesclun	3 to 8 weeks	Salsify and			
Okra	16 weeks	scorzonera	25 weeks		
Potato (early)	13 to 16 weeks	Shallot	18 to 26 weeks		
Radish	3 to 12 weeks	Swede	20 to 24 weeks		
Salad onion	10 weeks	Tomatillo	18 weeks		
Spinach	8 to 14 weeks				
Sweet corn	14 weeks				
Swiss chard	12 weeks				
Tomato	16 weeks				
Turnip	6 to 12 weeks				

Asparagus needs to grow a considerable length of time before you can harvest the spears.

All about seeds

Seeds are plants in waiting. All they need are the right triggers such as moisture and warmth to start growing.

A seed contains an embryonic plant in a dormant state, plus a reserve of energy to tide the new seedling over until it has developed sufficiently to fend for itself. The seed will remain dormant, protected by its outer casing, until the germination process is triggered by both moisture and warmth.

Importance of size

Once you open half a dozen packets of vegetable seeds, you will appreciate how widely they vary in size and appearance, and this will dictate how you sow them. Big, chunky runner bean seeds, for example, are easy to place individually at the correct spacing. However, tiny carrot seeds must be sown in a thin stream, and the resulting seedlings need to be thinned out to the right spacing later.

Seed size also affects sowing depth. Food reserves in the seed keep the seedling going from the moment of germination until the seedling breaks through the soil surface into the light. The larger the seed, the more reserves it contains. If a tiny seed is sown too deeply, its meagre food supply will run out before it manages to fight its way up through the soil.

Buying seeds

Seeds are available from every garden centre in the spring, but a much bigger selection is available from mail-order catalogues and Internet sites that specialise in selling seeds. The seed catalogues usually appear in late autumn or early winter, and they are nearly always free and contain a wealth of information. Look for advertisements in gardening magazines; once you're on the mailing list, the catalogue will usually keep coming every year.

What's on the packet?

Many seed packets have a colour picture on the front of the variety they contain – these pictures are always useful guides. However, you shouldn't reject packets from seed companies that don't produce colour pictures. These companies often stock less common varieties, and they may also provide more seeds in a packet, so you'll get more for your money.

Along with the type of vegetable, the seed packet should also provide a variety name such as bean 'Romano', lettuce 'Buttercrunch' or beet 'Boltardy'. There are international standards for plant names to ensure that the same variety is not available

CHECKING SEEDS FOR VIABILITY

If you have seeds that are a few years old and you're not sure if they are worth sowing, you can try this test:

Place a folded paper towel in the base of a wide-mouth cup or dish and moisten it. Place 10 seeds on the moist paper towel, put the dish in a plastic bag and seal it. Place the dish in a warm, dark place: a 21°C (70°F) temperature is ideal.

Check every other day that the paper towel is still moist, and after 10 days, count the number of seeds that have germinated. If the number is five or less, throw the seeds away. If it is six or seven, sow the seeds only if they are expensive or difficult to replace. If 8 to 10 seeds germinate, they are fine.

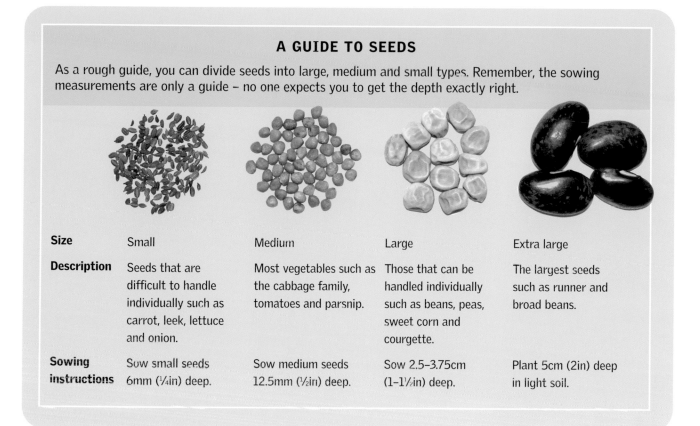

A GUIDE TO SEEDS

As a rough guide, you can divide seeds into large, medium and small types. Remember, the sowing measurements are only a guide – no one expects you to get the depth exactly right.

Size	Small	Medium	Large	Extra large
Description	Seeds that are difficult to handle individually such as carrot, leek, lettuce and onion.	Most vegetables such as the cabbage family, tomatoes and parsnip.	Those that can be handled individually such as beans, peas, sweet corn and courgette.	The largest seeds such as runner and broad beans.
Sowing instructions	Sow small seeds 6mm (¼in) deep.	Sow medium seeds 12.5mm (½in) deep.	Sow 2.5–3.75cm (1–1½in) deep.	Plant 5cm (2in) deep in light soil.

under several different names. The accepted way of writing a variety name is to enclose it between single quotation marks; however, this is not always practised on seed packets or in catalogues.

Many varieties are labelled as 'F1 hybrids'. This means that they are the first generation of seeds from a deliberate cross between two different-named varieties. F1 hybrids are often more vigorous and produce heavier, more uniform crops. These seeds are usually also more expensive than 'open-pollinated' varieties – plants whose flowers have been fertilised by those of the same variety while growing in the field.

Seed packets will usually inform you of the year the seeds were packed. There may also be instructions for sowing the seeds and growing the plants. However, these are often generalised, and you will probably need to adapt them for your particular garden, although some seed companies do provide detailed information on their packets.

The packet may sometimes say that it contains 'treated' seeds. This means that the seeds are particularly prone to pest or disease attack, so they have been pretreated with a fungicide or pesticide for improved germination. The seeds are dyed to make this treatment obvious, and you should wear gloves whenever you handle them. If you want to use only organic gardening methods you may prefer to avoid these seeds.

Storing seeds

If vegetable seeds are kept cool and dry, they can remain dormant but viable (capable of germination) for a number of years. However, for most vegetables, the fresher the seeds, the better the result. Old seeds germinate more slowly and patchily, and they may completely fail.

Store seeds in a cool, dark place, preferably in a sealed container with a sachet of silica gel to absorb any moisture. Also take note of the 'best before' date, which should be stamped on the packet. As a guide, five years is the maximum storage time for most vegetable seeds: onion, parsnip and sweet corn have much shorter lives and will remain viable for only a year or two.

Quick Tip

Shallow truth

Lettuce is unusual in that the seeds need light to be able to germinate, so it is particularly important to avoid burying lettuce seeds too deeply.

Preparing your plot for sowing

Many vegetable crops are sown outside, directly in the positions where they will mature, so it's worthwhile spending some time getting the vegetable plot into the ideal condition for the seeds.

STONY SOIL

Stony soil can be a nuisance because stones can make it difficult to draw a drill and sow evenly. However, if you rake away stones too energetically, you may bring more stones from below the surface up to the top.

Lightly rake the uppermost stones from the soil surface, gathering them with short strokes. Pick the stones off the soil and save them for another use such as making a path.

Frosty surprise

Quick Tip

Don't be tempted to start work too early in the year. An early warm break in the weather that makes you think spring is here can be followed by a return to winter conditions. Be guided by the average dates of the last frost in your particular region.

Most vegetables are sown in spring (although there are some vegetables sown outdoors in summer and autumn). For these spring-time sowings, prepare the soil in your vegetable plot in the autumn (see pages 30–43), so that winter frosts can help loosen the soil before sowing time arrives. However, you'll still have to add some final touches.

Reasons for a fine tilth

The object of working the soil for spring sowings is to break it down to a fine tilth – that means reducing the texture to small, even crumbs. If you sow seeds into rough soil full of clods, the seeds will end up at varying depths and not always with good access to soil moisture. This will lead to uneven germination – not to mention the practical difficulties of trying to draw a straight drill in lumpy soil.

Seeds are much easier to sow in a fine, crumbly soil where they can be covered to a consistent depth. The seeds will germinate much

Preparing the surface

If you dug over your plot in the autumn (see pages 40–41), you may need only a rake to prepare the surface of your soil for sowing. Alternatively, you may need to turn the plot over with a garden fork and break up large clods into a suitable size for raking. If the soil is wet wait until it has dried. When you can walk over the soil without it clinging to your boots, you know it's ready for you to start work.

1 If necessary turn over the soil and break up any large clods using a fork or a hoe; then begin levelling the soil with a rake.

more rapidly and consistently, and the seedlings will be able to push straight up through the soil crumbs instead of having to find their way round the clods.

When to prepare

If the soil is wet don't try to prepare it for sowing – it won't break down properly. You should wait until there are several fine, dry days, preferably with a brisk wind, which will help dry out the surface.

If you have a heavy soil such as clay that is always wet and difficult to work in spring, you can use cloches from late winter onwards to cover an area where you want to sow early crops. This will keep the soil dry and allow you to rake it down for sowing earlier than normal in the spring.

Assessing the soil

The amount of work needed to get soil in the right condition for sowing varies from garden to garden and from year to year. If you finish all your autumn digging on time, have a reasonably light soil and have a winter with lots of freezing and thawing to help break up the soil, you may need

only a rake to prepare the surface for sowing. If you're not so lucky you may need to turn the plot over with a garden fork to break up large clods into a suitable size for raking, but even this should be fairly light, quick work.

Creating a fine tilth

Once all the clods are broken down to pieces no bigger than the size of a fist, it's time to start raking. Raking removes stones and the remains of weeds, reduces the soil to fine crumbs and levels the surface of the plot. It is something of an art, but it's an art that's easily achieved with practise.

After levelling, it's a good idea to firm the bed, particularly if the soil is light in texture. You can do this simply by treading across the soil, using a rapid, shuffling gait that may bring a few strange looks from the neighbours but that is efficient at firming the entire soil surface evenly.

Once the plot is levelled and firmed, it's time to use a metal rake to achieve the final fine tilth. Work the rake lightly, with long, sweeping strokes. Break up any stubborn remaining clods with a sharp blow from the back of the rake.

2 As you level the soil, you can break up any large clods of soil into tiny pieces with the back of your rake, using a good sharp wallop.

3 After levelling the soil, firm it by treading across the plot. However, for heavy soil firm lightly with the palm of your hands instead.

4 Create the final fine tilth with a rake, using long, sweeping strokes and applying light pressure until all the soil is ready for sowing

Sowing seeds outdoors

Many vegetables are sown directly outdoors, where they will grow and can be harvested. Sowing in rows is the most common method, but there are other ways that can sometimes work better.

The usual way to sow seeds is in parallel rows across the vegetable garden. Mark out the position of the first row with a garden line – a piece of twine stretched taut between two sticks. For a shorter row you can use a length of wood as a guide.

Making a drill

Use the corner of a draw hoe to pull out a drill. To make sure the row is straight, place one foot on the line to hold it in the correct position as you make the drill. (For the correct depth of the drill see pages 50–51.)

If the soil is dry water the base of the drill before sowing. Take care to use a gentle stream of water. You can use a light dribble from a hose or create a gentle stream by putting your thumb partially over the spout of a watering can.

Sowing seeds in a drill

Try to space the seeds evenly as you sow them along the drill. You can tip some seeds out into the palm of one hand and take pinches of them to sprinkle along the row, or you might prefer to tap them carefully straight

out of the packet. (Creasing the edge of the packet to form a funnel will give you more control over the flow of seeds.) Some people prefer handheld seed sowers, which can be bought inexpensively from garden centres or mail-order catalogues.

Use whatever method you feel most comfortable with, as long as you're able to sow the seeds thinly and evenly. Small seeds such as carrots and lettuce are usually sown along the whole length of the row – and the seedlings are then thinned out to the correct spacing later.

Larger seeds are easier to handle, so you can sow them at their final spacing from the beginning – this is known as sowing at stations, and it uses fewer seeds. You can use this technique for crops such as French beans, parsnips and beets. To allow for germination failures sow three seeds at each station – weed out the surplus seedlings later.

Another method is to sow seeds at half their final spacing – for example, if you are growing beans 15cm (6in) apart, you can sow the seeds 8cm (3in) apart, then remove the surplus seedlings later. These extra seedlings are often useful for

Using the corner of a draw hoe, pull out a shallow drill in the soil along a taut garden line. Try to keep the drill an even depth.

Sow the seeds evenly along the length of the drill, whether you tap them straight out of the packet or use another method.

To make a double row, use the full width of the blade of a draw hoe to make a wide drill in the soil. Alternatively, you can use a spade to lift out the soil.

transplanting to fill up any gaps in the rest of the row.

Once the seeds are sown, cover them with soil as soon as each row is completed. Use a metal rake to pull the soil back to fill the drill evenly, being careful not to disturb the seeds. Finally, firm the soil, either by walking along the drill or tamping it down with the back of the rake. Label the

To make a shallow drill for small seeds, lay a rake along the soil where you want your row to grow. The handle of the rake will leave a depression that you can use as a drill.

Sow the seeds in two rows along each side of the drill. Alternatively, you can broadcast, or scatter, the seeds over the base of the drill.

row with the variety and the date of sowing, and move the garden line into position for the next row.

Other ways of sowing

Sowing in drills across the vegetable garden is convenient, but there are other methods that can work better.

Short rows. It is often impractical to harvest and use a whole, long row of a single crop such as lettuce before it goes to seed: in these cases, it can be more sensible to sow short rows. You should consider splitting a row into three sections and sowing them with different vegetables — for example, one-third with lettuce, one-third with radish and one-third with spring onions.

Wide rows. Peas are usually sown in drills about 15–20cm (6–8in) wide. Use a garden line or length of wood to guide a draw hoe or spade to make the drill. You can broadcast the peas over the base of the drill or sow them in two rows (see above). You can also use these wide rows for patches of lettuce and mesclun crops.

Broadcast. Instead of sowing seeds in drills, you can broadcast them by scattering the seeds over an area of soil in the same way you would sow a lawn. Some crops such as lettuce are sown with this technique in little

square beds, but it makes controlling weeds difficult. As an alternative to broadcasting, sow seeds in closely spaced, short rows within the beds. It is then easy to distinguish between crop seedlings and weed seedlings when they emerge, and you can use the hoe or hand weed until the crop plants grow large enough to cover the whole bed.

Individual spacing. You can sow large seeds — runner beans, for example — by simply pushing them into the soil instead of drawing a drill, which can save time. You can use a dibber to make the hole for the seeds, but first mark the depth on the dibber so that you can ensure you sow the seeds at the correct depth.

Mounds. Squashes do well when they are sown on a little hill of soil. The necks of the plants are prone to rot if they are surrounded by moisture, and sowing on a hill ensures the water can drain away from the stems. Draw the soil up into a mound, and sow three seeds into the top. Make a moatlike channel circling around the base of the mound, which will divert water to the roots, where it will be needed.

When mounding seeds, draw the soil up into a mound about 10cm (4in) high and 20cm (8in) across; then sow three seeds into the top of the mound.

Special sowing techniques

Seeds usually germinate easily, but there are times when a little extra help is required. There are several ways of making sure you get the best results from your sowings.

For seeds that are slow or difficult to germinate try a technique known as fluid sowing. It is also a good technique if you are sowing early in the spring, when weather and soil conditions are unpredictable.

The technique involves first pre-germinating the seeds in a warm place indoors and then mixing them with a carrier gel before 'sowing' them in the garden. Because germination has already taken place, the seeds grow quickly, even if in cold soil. Fluid sowing is useful for slow-germinating seeds such as parsley, parsnips and celery and in short-season areas for carrots and other root crops, lettuce and cabbages.

Steps to fluid sowing

To prepare the seeds first line the inside of a plastic sandwich container with paper towel. Moisten the paper towel thoroughly before scattering the seeds thinly over it. Cover the container and keep it at 21°C (70°F). Check the container every couple of days; as soon as most of the seeds show signs of germination, it is time to sow them. The emerging roots should be only just visible (you will need a magnifying glass for small seeds); if they are allowed to develop too far the process will fail.

Make a gel to carry the seeds. Use a wallpaper paste (choose a fungicide-free one) diluted 50 per cent with water, or mix 30–45ml (2–3tbsp) of cornflour with 575ml (1pt) of boiling water and allow it to cool. Make the gel thick enough so the seeds remain suspended and don't sink.

Wash the pre-germinated seeds off the paper towel into a sieve with a gentle stream of water and then stir them into the gel with your fingers until they are well distributed. Put the gel into a plastic bag, snip off one corner and squeeze the gel into an already prepared, moistened drill. Cover the seeds as usual.

Pelleted seeds

Seeds that are individually coated with a clay compound that sets hard are

Stale seedbed

This technique helps to prevent annual weeds from swamping your seedlings. Allow weed seeds buried in the top of the soil to germinate, then destroy them before planting vegetable seeds. When you destroy the weeds, be careful to do so in a way that does not disturb the soil any further.

1 Prepare the seedbed about two to three weeks before you want to sow your vegetables, then wait.

2 Within a short time there will be a flush of weeds from the seeds that have been brought close to the surface by your cultivation.

To use a seed tape cut it to the appropriate length, place it at the bottom of a drill and cover it with soil.

known as pelleted seeds. The hard coating makes the seeds larger and evenly rounded, so they are easier to handle and space accurately. Some seed coatings include nutrients or fungicides. Pelleted seeds do not necessarily germinate more quickly – in fact, they may germinate more slowly. Keep the soil moist after sowing to allow the clay coat to break down.

Seed tapes

Small seeds are sometimes glued onto long, thin strips of paper at the correct spacing – these are called seed tapes. Simply lay a length of tape along the base of a drill and cover it with soil. The paper will rot away, and the seedlings will emerge perfectly spaced and in nice straight rows.

You can make your own seed tape using strips of 2.5cm (1in)-wide plain paper such as photocopy paper or newspaper. Make a glue by mixing together flour and water until the mixture is the consistency of gravy. Use a small artist's paintbrush to dab a dot of glue at regular intervals along the paper at the appropriate spacing for the seeds: gently place the seeds on the glue. Allow the glue to dry.

Catch crops

Some crops are slow to germinate and develop. To make maximum use of space in your vegetable garden you can plant quick-growing 'catch crops' in between them. You'll harvest the quicker-growing crop before it starts to compete with the slower one.

A classic combination is parsnips and radishes. Parsnips can take 28 days to germinate, whereas radishes need less than a week. Sow the parsnips at appropriately spaced stations (see pages 54–55) and sprinkle radish seeds in a drill in between each station. Cover the seeds as usual. You will be able to start eating the radishes before they interfere with the parsnip seedlings. The radishes will also help prevent a cap, or crust, from forming on

the soil, which allows the germinating parsnips to push through more easily.

Other slow-germinating crops include beets, Swiss chard, endive, leeks, onions and parsley. For catch crops try spinach and lettuce. You can also try successional cropping (see page 18).

HOT WEATHER TIPS

Most seeds need warmth to germinate. However, for many vegetables, germination will be hampered if temperatures reach above 30°C (86°F). Lettuce seeds are especially vulnerable. They become dormant at soil temperatures above 25°C (78°F).

The timing of sowing is essential; for example, sow lettuce seeds in the early afternoon during hot spells, so that the critical germination process is most likely to take place during the coolness of night time. You should water the bottom of the seed drills immediately before sowing to keep the temperature down.

In countries with consistently high temperatures the problem is often resolved by pre-germinating the seeds under controlled, cooler conditions indoors and then using the fluid-sowing technique or transplant the seedlings (see pages 68–69).

3 Careful hoeing, using a sharp blade that slices off the weeds at the soil surface, will kill the weeds, or use a flame gun or herbicides.

4 As soon as the weeds are gone, you can sow the vegetable seeds with as little soil disturbance as possible.

Quick Tip

Marker crops

The catch-crop technique is useful as a marker to show where a slow-germinating row has been sown. You'll appreciate this marker when you need to weed between the rows before the slow-growing seedlings appear.

Care after sowing

A newly emerged seedling is very vulnerable, but a little special care will ensure that it soon develops into a strong and healthy young plant.

During the first stage of the germination process, the seed absorbs water from the surrounding soil, which softens the seed coat so that the young root can emerge. Part of the reason for breaking the soil down into fine crumbs is to ensure that the seed will be in contact with sufficient soil moisture for this process to happen. The process can take from one or two days to several weeks, depending on the type of seed.

The emerging seed

Once the seed absorbs enough water, and if the soil temperature is suitable, an embryonic root known as the radicle will grow. No matter which way the seed is positioned, the radicle will grow downwards, guided by a positive response to gravity. Fine root hairs develop on the rapidly growing root, and these absorb water and minerals from the soil. The root helps to anchor the plant in the ground.

Shortly after root growth begins, the seed's shoot starts to develop. The tip of the shoot – the plumule – is held between two bulky seed leaves, or cotyledons, which help to protect the plumule as it pushes through the soil. The shoot responds to gravity, but with a negative response, growing in the opposite direction to gravity.

While the seedling is growing up through the soil, it relies on the food stored in the seed leaves. The leaves start to photosynthesise to make energy from sunlight only when the seedling breaks through the soil surface. Bury a seed too deeply, and its food supply may run out before the seedling reaches the surface.

Seedlings can push past small obstacles in the soil. However, if they hit a larger obstacle such as a stone, they have to find a way round it before they can continue towards the surface. A fine, light, crumbly soil, free from stones and other debris, makes life easier for the seedlings, helping them to reach daylight quickly.

Providing the right conditions

Make sure you keep the soil moist, but not flooded, at all times after sowing. Watering the drill before sowing is the best way to supply moisture, but if conditions are extremely dry in the following days, additional watering may be necessary before the seedlings emerge.

Be sure to water using a watering can with a rose or a sprinkler to give a fine spray; a jet of water is likely to wash the seeds out of the soil. Heavy droplets can also cause the surface layer of soil to form a hard cap, or crust, as

The first true leaves are above the cotyledons on top of the stem.

The seedling grows upwards with new leaves, while the roots continue to spread.

The cotyledons and plumule push up from the soil.

The radicle breaks through the seed coat, and root hairs appear.

Thinning

Seedlings will need thinning once they are large enough to handle easily but before they start to crowd one another. Select the strongest seedlings to leave in place at the appropriate spacing, and carefully remove all the others.

1 If your plants are not growing closely together, you can slice off the extra seedlings with a sharp hoe blade.

2 To remove nearby seedlings hold the remaining plant with a finger at each side; push down as you tug away the others.

3 You can use the extra thinnings by carefully planting them in a less crowded area in the plot. You should hold them by their leaves.

4 After thinning, water the seedlings using a watering can with a fine rose or a fine spray from a hose.

it dries, which the seedlings might not be able to penetrate. Capping is a particular problem on fine, silty or clay soil. Covering moist soil with finely shredded bark, a single sheet of wet newspaper or horticultural fleece will help keep the moisture in and prevent a cap from forming. Make sure you remove the paper or fleece once the seedlings emerge, before it restricts their growth.

Soil temperature is more difficult to control than moisture, so getting the timing of sowing right is the most important factor. If a sudden, unexpected cold spell arrives after sowing, you can use horticularal fleece, cloches or plastic tunnels to protect the seedbed from the worst of the weather.

After germination, continue to keep the soil moist, but make sure you still use the fine spray to avoid damaging the young plants.

Thinning

Seeds are sown relatively thickly to allow for inevitable germination failures. Once the seedlings are through the soil, they will grow quickly and you will soon find them competing for space. At this point, the young plants usually require thinning to the recommended spacing.

It is often a good idea to carry out thinning in two stages. If the final spacing required is 15cm (6in), thin the seedlings first to 8cm (3in) apart, then to their final spacing a few weeks later. This helps to avoid gaps in the row where selected seedlings have died.

PEST CONTROL

Some pests are attracted to plants by the scent produced by their bruised foliage – this is how the carrot fly, for example, finds its targets. Thinning out seedlings will release a strong scent, so you should do your thinning shortly before dusk, giving the adult flies minimal time to track down the source.

You can help disguise the scent by growing a strong-smelling herb such as rue or chamomile near your plants. However, don't grow parsley, which is related to carrots and is also attractive to carrot flies.

A guide to sowing seeds

This chart is a quick at-a-glance guide to basic sowing information. For detailed information see the full entries for each vegetable.

Vegetable	When to sow	Spacing (between rows)	Spacing (within rows)	Comments
Beetroot pages 194–95	Early to late spring; again in midsummer	45cm (18in)	10–15cm (4–6in)	Intensive spacing: sow thinly over a 30–45cm (15–18in)-wide bed.
Broccoli rabe page 175	Early to mid-spring	45cm (18in)	15cm (6in)	Can broadcast seeds in wide rows; thin to 7.5cm (3in) for intensive spacing.
Broad beans pages 148–49	After all danger of frost is past	45–75cm (18–30in)	15cm (6in)	Intensive spacing: 15cm (6in) apart on centre.
Carrots pages 192–93	Early spring to late summer	15–30cm (6–12in)	5–10cm (2–4in)	Sow seeds every 3 weeks if you want a succession crop.
Celeriac page 201	Early spring	60cm (24in)	20–25cm (8–10in)	Intensive spacing: 30cm (12in) apart on centre.
Chicory page 134	Early to mid-spring; again in midsummer	45–60cm (18–24in); for grumolo 30cm (12in)	25–30cm (10–12in); for grumolo 15–20cm (6–8in)	In hot-summer areas sow to avoid leaves maturing in peak heat.

Vegetable	When to sow	Spacing (between rows)	Spacing (within rows)	Comments
Climbing beans pages 150–53	After all danger of frost is past	Double rows: 60cm (2ft) apart, 1.5m (5ft) between rows	15–23cm (6–9in)	Or sow seeds at the base of stakes or tepee poles; thin plants.
Courgettes and marrows pages 226–27	Early summer, after all danger of frost is past	60–90cm (24–36in)	60–90cm (24–36in)	In cold areas raise seeds under cover.
Kohlrabi page 179	Mid-spring to late summer	30–90cm (12–36in)	15cm (6in)	Sow seeds every 2 weeks for a succession crop.
Lettuce pages 128–31	Early spring until autumn	45–60cm (18–24in)	15–30cm (6–12in)	Try to time the sowing to avoid the hottest periods of the summer.
Melons pages 234–37	After all danger of frost is past	1.2–1.8m (4–6ft); for watermelon, 1.5–2.1m (5–7ft)	1.2–1.8m (4–6ft); for watermelon, 1.5–2.1m (5–7ft)	Raise seeds in a heated greenhouse or propagator.
Mesclun pages 136–37	Early spring until autumn	7.5–15cm (3–6in)	Sow lightly	Alternatively, you can broadcast seeds lightly over a wide row.
Okra pages 220–21	Early to mid-spring	45–90cm (18–36in)	30–60cm (12–24in)	Raise seeds in a heated greenhouse or propagator.
Onions pages 158–61	Early to mid-spring or autumn	30–45cm (12–18in)	10–15cm (4–6in)	For salad onions sow thinly and harvest without thinning.
Parsnips page 197	Early spring	45–60cm (18–24in)	10–15cm (4–6in)	Seeds are slow to germinate.

(Continued)

Vegetable	When to sow	Spacing (between rows)	Spacing (within rows)	Comments
Peas pages 144–47	Early spring to mid-summer	60cm (24in)	10–15cm (4–6in)	Choose different varieties to harvest over a longer period.
Pumpkins and winter squash pages 228–33	Early summer, after all danger of frost is past	1.50–1.8m (5–6ft)	1.8m (6ft); compact varieties, 0.6–1.2m (2–4ft)	Raise seeds under cover.
Radishes page 196	Early spring through to mid-summer	15cm (6in)	5–10cm (2–4in)	You can sow seeds in succession throughout the season.
Rocket page 132	Early to mid-spring; again in late summer	15cm (6in)	2.5–15cm (1–6in)	Close spacing provides baby leaves for harvesting.
Salsify and scorzonera page 202	Early spring	38–45cm (15–18in)	10–15cm (4–6in)	Keep the grassy seedlings weed-free.
Spinach pages 138–39	Early spring; again in mid- to late summer	45cm (18in)	10–15cm (4–6in)	You can sow seeds later to overwinter for a spring harvest.
Sweet corn pages 240–43	After danger of last spring frost is past	90cm (36in)	7.5–10cm (3–4in)	Plant in blocks of at least 4 rows to ensure pollination.
Swiss chard pages 140–41	Early spring and again in mid- to late summer	30–60cm (12–24in)	15–30cm (6–12in)	Less likely to bolt than spinach during hot weather.
Turnips pages 198–99	Early spring and again in mid-summer to autumn	45cm (18in)	2.5–15cm (1–6in)	Space close to harvest greens; use wider spacings for roots.

Starting transplants

While many vegetable crops are left to mature where they are sown, others are moved to new positions as young plants. There are several reasons why this may be a good idea – and there are some occasions when it is a bad one.

(For more information about sowing in seedbeds see pages 66–67.)

PROPAGATORS

Heated propagators are special units for raising seeds and cuttings; they supply a gentle warmth to the sowing compost, which helps ensure quick, even germination and rooting. An electric cable runs through the base of the propagator and can be thermostatically controlled to achieve the ideal level of heat. Seed trays filled with compost and sown in the traditional way are placed on top of the heated base.

Some propagators are supplied with their own covers to keep humidity levels high; if not you should fit each tray with its own individual plastic propagator top.

Starting plants off in one spot and moving them to another saves wasting space in the vegetable garden. Brussels sprouts, for example, need plenty of space as they mature, but as seedlings and young plants, they are happy growing close together. Starting them in a separate seedbed allows the area earmarked for their final positions to be used for a fast-growing crop while the sprouts are still in their early stages. (For more information about sowing in seedbeds see pages 66–67.)

Starting under cover

Sometimes seeds are sown indoors, in a heated propagator or greenhouse, or under cover outdoors earlier than they can be sown outside, and then transplanted to their final growing position. This gives the plants a good start, and in cooler areas it enables

You can sow large seeds in individual compartments in a seed tray filled with a sterile sowing compost.

Growing seedlings don't need such a humid atmosphere – too much humidity encourages fungus diseases such as damping-off.

When pricking out, handle the seedlings by their seed leaves (the first, expendable pair of leaves that open). Never touch the stems.

give them more room to develop, and this is known as pricking out. They can be spaced farther apart in another tray or moved to individual pots.

Prick out seedlings as soon as they are large enough to handle. Use a dibber to lever the roots carefully out of the compost: you may need to lever up a small clump of seedlings and gently untangle the roots. Make a hole with the dibber in the new container of sowing compost; then lower the seedling into it, making sure the roots make contact with the base of the hole and are not dangling in midair. Firm the seedling in gently.

When the container is planted, water it, using a fine rose, and put it in a well-shaded place. The seedlings often droop after pricking out, but after a few hours they should recover and you can bring them into the light.

earlier harvesting than would otherwise be possible. Starting seeds under cover is also good for seeds that are difficult to germinate such as celery and for types that are difficult to find or are expensive. When sown in containers under cover, it is easier to provide them with the best conditions for germination than when sown outside.

Sowing in containers

You can sow seeds for transplanting in trays or pots, according to the type of plant and the size of seeds. Use a sterile sowing compost to avoid problems with weeds and soil-borne pests and diseases often found in garden soil. Fill the seed tray or pot evenly, pushing the compost out to the corners of the tray, and level it off and firm it with a presser. Water the compost, using a fine rose on the watering can; then allow it to drain for an hour or so before sowing.

Space large seeds by hand; shake out smaller seeds thinly and evenly over the surface of the compost. Cover the seeds with more sowing compost to the

recommended depth; you can shake the compost through a small garden sieve for an even distribution. Cover the containers with plastic propagator tops, a sheet of glass or an upturned seed tray to keep in the moisture and warmth. Add a sheet of newspaper on top of a transparent cover.

Keep the seeds in an even warmth (check the packets for the suggested germination temperature) and keep the compost just moist. Once the first seedlings appear, remove the newspaper or upturned tray to allow light to reach the plants; when the first seedlings reach the glass cover remove that too. Propagator tops have extra headroom, so they can be left on the trays or pots for longer, but when all the seedlings appear open the ventilators or prop the cover up for good air circulation. When watering is necessary use a fine rose to avoid damage and keep the compost moist, never wet.

Pricking out

If the seeds were well spaced or individually sown, the young plants may be able to remain in the same containers until it is time to plant them in their final positions. However, most seedlings will need replanting to

TRANSPLANTING PROBLEMS

Transplanting often involves damage to the roots and gives the plants a slight 'check' to their growth. For this reason it is not a good idea to transplant root crops such as parsnips, salsify, scorzonera and carrots, because any damage to the young root will cause it to be misshapen at maturity.

Root disturbance can also cause susceptible crops to bolt, or run to seed, prematurely – Florence fennel, spinach, lettuce and Chinese cabbage are often affected in this way.

However, it is still possible to transplant these difficult plants. You can sow individual seeds in soil blocks or in fibre pots, which can be planted in their entirety to avoid root disturbance.

Starting transplants in seedbeds

You can sow vegetables that don't need the extra protection of a greenhouse in an outdoor seedbed, then transplant them to their final positions at a later date.

There are two main vegetable candidates for sowing in a seedbed: the members of the brassica, or cabbage, family – particularly those that mature in the winter and spring – and leeks. Sowing them in seedbeds avoids wasting space in the garden. (For vegetables that shouldn't be transplanted see page 65.)

Determining the size of the bed

The size of your seedbed will depend on the number of plants you intend to grow. As a rough guide, most cabbage-family plants will require a final spacing of about 60cm (24in) apart. You can thin seedlings in the seedbed to 5cm (2in) apart and grow them in rows 15cm (6in) apart. This means that a seedbed row 60cm (24in) long should provide enough young plants for a crop row that is 7m (24ft) long.

Preparing the soil

You should prepare the soil as you would for sowing into the vegetable garden (see pages 52–53). An advantage of a seedbed is that it

Making a seedbed

Ideally, choose a site where the seedbed will be in a sheltered position. The soil should be fertile and easily worked so that you can prepare a fine tilth.

1 To mark out the area for your seedbed, you can use twine held in place by stakes at each corner.

is a small area, which is much easier to get it into an ideal condition for raising seedlings. Add plenty of well-rotted compost or similar organic material in the autumn, and rake the soil to a fine tilth in early spring. Cabbage-family plants prefer a firm soil, so remember to tamp the seedbed area thoroughly.

Sowing the seeds

Because the seedbed is usually small, it is not normally necessary to use a line for sowing. Instead, press the handle of a hoe or rake into the soil to make a drill. On heavy soil, this may compress the soil too much; instead, lay a tool handle on the ground as the guide and pull out the drill with a hoe in the usual way.

Sow the seeds thinly along the drills. Because the seedlings will be transplanted, some root damage is bound to occur, but thin sowing will help prevent a tangle of roots and keep the damage to a minimum.

When sowing several different types of cabbage-family plants, you should label each drill as soon as it is sown. Otherwise you'll find that trying to distinguish between rows

of almost identical-looking cabbage, cauliflower and Brussels sprout seedlings is not easy.

Caring for the seedlings

Cabbage-family plants will usually germinate within 7 to 14 days; leeks take a little longer at 21 to 25 days. Once the seedlings emerge, keep the soil moist by watering through a fine rose. The object is to keep the young plants growing without any interruption to their growth.

When cabbage-family seedlings are large enough to handle, thin them to 3–5cm (1–2in) apart. Slender leek seedlings do not usually need thinning as long as they have been sown reasonably thinly.

Cabbage-family plants will be ready for transplanting after five to seven weeks, when the plants are about 10–15cm (4–6in) high. Try not to delay any longer; the larger the plants, the more of a growth check they will receive. You can transplant leeks when they grow to about 15–20cm (6–8in) tall – usually about 8 to 10 weeks after sowing – when their stems are about half the thickness of a pencil.

BUYING TRANSPLANTS

If you don't have the space or time to raise your own plants from seeds, you can buy young plants for transplanting from garden centres and mail-order suppliers. They are available either as bare-root plants that have been lifted from the open soil or plug plants, or (more expensively) as plants growing in containers of various sizes.

Make sure that bare-root plants look fresh and healthy, and that their roots have been carefully wrapped to protect them from drying out while you bring them home. As soon as you get home dunk them in a bucket of water and plant them without delay.

When buying cabbage-family seedlings, be aware that you can import incurable club-root disease into your garden. If possible always raise your own seedlings. If you buy transplants ask your supplier if they have been raised in sterile compost. If not you shouldn't buy them.

2 After preparing the soil, lay the handle of a garden rake or fork on the ground and step on it to form the drills.

3 Sow the seeds thinly along each drill. Remember to label each drill so you can identify the young seedlings.

4 Cover the seedlings with a thin layer of soil: without pushing it down, use a rake to move the soil at right angles to the drill.

Planting out transplants

It's important to plant out young vegetables as soon as they are ready – a delay could reduce both the quality and quantity of the harvest. You also need to take steps to reduce the stress on transplants as much as possible.

If you delay the transplant of cabbage-family plants for only two or three weeks, you will reduce both the yield and the quality of the crop, because of the greater stress suffered by larger transplants. (To determine when they are ready for transplanting, see pages 66–67.) This is also true for other vegetables that have been grown under cover, although some vegetables such as leeks are less sensitive to transplanting.

Hardening off

If young plants have been raised under cover indoors, in a greenhouse or in a frame, they must be hardened off – gradually acclimatised to the cooler temperatures in the open garden – before they will be ready for planting

in their final positions. Moving them straight from a warm environment to one that is several degrees colder will seriously affect their growth, sometimes to such an extent that you will lose any advantage of an early start.

Hardening off should take about two weeks. First increase the amount of ventilation the vegetables receive under cover; then move them to a sheltered position outside during the day, bringing them under cover again in the evening. After a few days, you can leave the plants in a sheltered spot outside all day and night; finally, move the plants from the shelter to an open position just before planting.

A frame is a useful adjunct to a heated greenhouse. Young plants can

start their hardening-off process in the closed frame, with more ventilation given day by day until the frame lights are left open entirely.

Choosing the day

The ideal weather for transplanting is overcast and still; a hot, sunny, breezy day will make it difficult for plants to recover from the inevitable wilting when they are newly planted. Wait a few days for better conditions, if possible, or tackle the job in the evening when it is cooler.

Preparation for planting

You should thoroughly prepare the designated area for planting. Although the soil does not have to be as fine as the tilth needed for sowing seeds, it should be raked down well and the soil should be crumbly to allow the plants to grow quickly.

A few days before transplanting, water the young plants thoroughly, ensuring the water penetrates to the plants' full rooting depth. This will help to reduce root damage when lifting the plants.

Before lifting the plants or knocking them out of their pots, make sure you have everything ready for planting –

Planting out

Before starting dig a hole the appropriate size for each vegetable plant with a trowel. Once a row has been completely planted, water the row, providing enough water to penetrate the whole rooting area.

1 Loosen the soil in the pot or tray by tapping the container. Tip up the container to help ease the plant out, and gently handle the plant by the soil ball – avoid holding it by the stem.

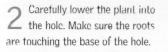

2 Carefully lower the plant into the hole. Make sure the roots are touching the base of the hole.

3 Fill in the hole with good-quality soil, and firm in the soil with the heel of your hand or by treading. Test that the plants are firm enough by tugging gently at a leaf – there should be no movement of the plant in the soil.

for example, put a straight line in position ready for the first row.

Preparing potted transplants

If a vegetable plant has been raised in an individual pot you should remove it from its container by turning the pot upside down, then, with the plant stem between your fore and second fingers, rap the top edge of the pot firmly on a hard surface. This should enable the root ball of the plant to slide out with minimum disturbance to the roots.

If young plants have been raised in trays, loosen the compost by shaking the tray firmly from side to side and tapping the base on a hard surface. Then prise up a section of the compost and carefully separate the plants, teasing the roots apart.

Preparing seedbed transplants

Try to minimise the time the seedlings are out of the soil. If you are lifting young plants from a seedbed, don't lift all the seedlings at once. Take only as many as you can plant and water within 20 minutes or so, then return for another batch.

To lift the plants push a fork deeply under the row of transplants and lever them up carefully. When transplanting cabbage-family plants you should handle them by their leaves to separate the individual plants, teasing the roots apart while trying to retain as much of the soil clinging to the roots as you can. Lay the plants in a tray and cover them with damp sacking or newspaper until you can plant them in their new positions.

CARING FOR TRANSPLANTS

The transplants will flag at first, but they will soon recover if they receive enough water. If the transplanting day is sunny lay a horticultural fleece or single sheets of newspaper over the top of the plants to shade them until the evening. To get the plants off to the best possible start, give them an application of a balanced liquid fertiliser immediately after planting. Continue to water as necessary over the following days.

A guide to transplanting

The following pages provide a quick reference on information for transplanting. For more detailed information see the full entries for each vegetable.

Vegetable	When to sow	When to transplant	Spacing (between rows)	Spacing (within rows)	Comments
Aubergines pages 218–19	Early to mid-spring under cover	Early to mid-summer, after all danger of frost is past	45–60cm (18–24in)	45–60cm (18–24in)	Aubergines do best grown to maturity in a greenhouse.
Broccoli page 174	Early spring through to mid-summer	Mid-spring and late summer	60cm (24in)	45cm (18in)	The sowing and cropping time will vary according to the varieties you choose.
Brussels sprouts pages 172–73	Early to mid-summer	Mid- to late summer	45cm (18in); for tall varieties, 60cm (24in)	45cm (18in); for tall varieties, 60cm (24in)	You can sow a range of varieties to harvest Brussels sprouts over a longer period.
Broad beans pages 148–49	Mid- to late spring under cover	Early summer, after all danger of frost is past	45–75cm (18–30in)	15cm (6in)	You can also sow broad beans in autumn if you live in a mild area.
Cabbage pages 170–71	Early spring to mid-summer	Mid-spring to late summer	45cm (18in); for small heads, 30cm (12in)	45cm (18in); for small heads, 30cm (12in)	With the right varieties, you can grow cabbages all year round.
Cauliflower pages 176–77	Early spring to early summer	Mid-spring to midsummer	60–90cm (24–36in); intensive spacing, 45cm (18in)	38–60cm (15–24in); intensive spacing, 45cm (18in)	Sowing and cropping times vary according to variety.

Vegetable	When to sow	When to transplant	Spacing (between rows)	Spacing (within rows)	Comments
Celeriac page 201	Early spring	Mid- to late spring	60cm (24in)	20–25cm (8–10in)	You can also plant celeriac 30cm (12in) apart on centre.
Celery page 200	Late winter to early spring	Mid- to late spring	60cm (24in)	23–30cm (9–12in)	You can also consider planting celery about 30cm (12in) apart on centre.
Climbing beans pages 150–53	Mid- to late spring under cover	Late spring to early summer, when all danger of frost is past	Double rows: 0.6m (2ft) apart, with 1.5m (5ft) between rows	15–23cm (6–9in)	Sowing climbing beans under cover will give you a longer cropping season.
Courgettes and marrow pages 226–27	Mid-spring under cover	After all danger of frost is past	60–90cm (24–36in)	60–90cm (24–36in)	To establish transplants cover with a tunnel or fleece.
Cucumbers pages 224–25	Early to mid-spring under cover	After danger of frost is past; in greenhouse, mid- to late spring	30cm (12in)	30cm (12in)	Or sow outdoors in mounds 90–120cm (3–4ft) apart.
Florence fennel page 203	In early spring under cover	Mid-spring	25–30cm (10–12in)	25–30cm (10–12in)	Sow varieties that are bolt resistant in modules or peat pots to minimise root disturbance.

(Continued)

Vegetable	When to sow	When to transplant	Spacing (between rows)	Spacing (within rows)	Comments
Kale page 178	Mid-spring to midsummer	Early to late summer	45cm (18in)	30–45cm (12–18in)	Firm the soil thoroughly on transplanting and water until established.
Kohlrabi page 179	Early to mid-spring	Mid- to late spring	30–90cm (12–36in)	15cm (6in)	Sow in modules to protect roots; transplant eary to avoid bolting.
Leeks pages 164–65	Late winter to early spring	Late spring to early summer	30–45 cm (12–18in)	10–15cm (4–6in)	Can sow indoors 10–12 weeks before outdoor planting date.
Lettuce pages 128–31	Late winter to early spring under cover	Mid-spring	45–60cm (18–24in)	15–30cm (6–12in)	When transplanting, handle the plants carefully to minimise root disturbance.
Melons pages 234–37	Mid-spring under cover	Late spring to early summer, after all danger of frost is past	1.2–1.8m (4–6ft)	1.2–1.8m (4–6ft)	Choose varieties suitable for cool climates.
Okra pages 220–21	Early to mid-spring under cover	Early to mid-summer, after all risk of frost is past	45–90cm (18–36in)	30–60cm (12–24in)	Use a black plastic mulch to warm the soil planting; handle transplants carefully to protect roots.

Vegetable	When to sow	When to transplant	Spacing (between rows)	Spacing (within rows)	Comments
Onions pages 158–61	Mid- to late winter under cover; autumn if overwintering	Spring or autumn	30–45cm (12–18in)	10–15cm (4–6in)	Make sure you choose the correct varieties for autum sowing.
Peppers pages 214–17	Early spring under cover	Late spring	60–90cm (24–36in)	38–45cm (15–18in)	In cool areas grow peppers to maturity in a greenhouse.
Pumpkins and winter squash pages 228–33	Mid-spring under cover	After all danger of frost is past	1.5–1.8m (5–6ft)	1.8m (6ft); for compact varieties, 0.6–1.2m (2–4ft)	Plant in mounds warmed by black plastic; protect the transplants from cold weather.
Sweet corn pages 240–43	Mid-spring under cover	After all danger of frost is past	90cm (36in)	25cm (10in) to 60cm (24in), depending on the variety	Sow short types in double rows 30cm (12in) apart.
Tomatillos pages 212–13	Early to mid-spring under cover	Mid-spring to early summer	60–90cm (24–36in)	60–90cm (24–36in)	In cool areas grow tomatillos to maturity in a greenhouse.
Tomatoes pages 206–11	Early to mid-spring under cover	Mid- to late spring and early summer	0.6–1.2m (2–4ft)	0.6–1.2m (2–4ft)	For best results in cool areas, grow tomatoes to maturity under cover in a greenhouse.

Extending the growing season

If the growing season is too short for all the crops you would like to grow, there are methods you can use to lengthen it, from simply mounding soil over potato shoots to protect them from late spring frosts to creating an indoor space to start seedlings.

These protective materials are made either from a lightweight, woven fabric or from a clear, perforated plastic film. You can lay them on top of growing crops without damaging them. Both types allow moisture and air through to the plants while providing a degree of protection from cold weather, as well as from insects and animals.

You should anchor horticultural fleece or film securely around the edges by digging them into the soil or weighing them down with stones. Although they stretch to an extent to accommodate growing crops, you will need to adjust them occasionally to prevent damage to the plants.

In cool and temperate regions you can extend the season by sowing seeds and growing seedlings early in the year, before spring arrives. However, warm-season vegetables such as tomatoes and peppers will not survive even a slight frost, and in many places frosts occur into mid-spring. Yet, if sowing seeds is delayed until all risk of frost has passed, the remaining season may be too short to allow the plants to reach maturity.

The answer is to provide protection to allow the seedlings to thrive. Even crops that are not frost-tender can benefit from being started under protection; the warmer conditions allow faster growth, giving plants under cover a head start over those sown outside, leading to earlier crops.

Areas where spring comes late often have to suffer the double blow of autumn and winter arriving early, too. However, plants that have not finished producing their crop by the time the autumn weather arrives can often be safeguarded against early frosts, wind and rain by using movable forms of protection, such as cloches and horticultural fleece. The extra days gained can make all the difference to your final harvest.

Simple forms of protection

If the forecast of a late, sharp spring frost takes you by surprise when potato shoots are thrusting through their ridges, or tender seedlings are beginning to show in their drills, don't panic. You can protect early potatoes by earthing them up every two or three weeks once the shoots appear. Carefully pull the soil over the top of the shoots with a draw hoe. This will protect them from frost damage and the shoots will soon push their way through the soil. Or you could use single sheets of newspaper or horticultural fleece laid over the

Piles of loose dry straw, leaves or compost can provide some insulation against cold weather in the autumn.

Horticultural fleece can be stretched over vegetable plants such as these carrots to provide protection from cold weather.

top of the shoots. This method also works well with newly germinated seedlings. Weight down the edges of the paper or fleece with soil to prevent it from being blown away.

The shoulders of root crops such as swedes, parsnips and carrots can be damaged by exposure to hard frost at the soil surface. Heaping dry leaves, straw or compost over the rows before cold weather sets in will give them protection, and it will make it easier to dig the crops up in freezing spells.

Heavy clay soil takes a long time to dry out and become fit to break down for sowing seeds. You can speed up the process of preparing the soil by covering it with cloches or sheets of sturdy black plastic from mid-winter onwards. This will keep off the rain and snow, allowing the soil to dry out and warm up. Black plastic is particularly good at retaining warmth.

Cloches

Early cloches were bell-shaped and made from heavy glass to fit over individual plants. Nowadays, cloches are available in many different types and styles. They are normally shaped so that they can be placed end to end to form a continuous cover over a row of plants.

Glass cloches provide excellent shelter from cold and wet weather, and they can raise the temperature of the air considerably, as long as the ends of the rows are blocked. They are also stable. However, glass has a number of drawbacks; it is fragile, dangerous when broken (a point to keep in mind if there are young children in the garden), expensive and heavy to move around. Cloches made from corrugated or sheet plastic are much cheaper and easier to move, but not quite as effective at trapping warmth. Remember that they need to be firmly anchored in place.

Cloches may be barn-shaped, tent-shaped or semi-circular. Check how much headroom the different types provide and whether it is sufficient for your plants.

Setting up an indoor space

Gardeners living in a region with a short growing season can still grow plants with a long growing season by starting them indoors, as long as they are provided with the correct conditions. The soil temperature needs to be warm enough for the seedlings to germinate – this will depend on

the type of vegetable you are growing – and you need to keep the soil moist.

Light is vitally important. If you don't have enough room on a sunny window sill, position a table near the window. Alternatively, clear a space elsewhere in the house and provide light for the plants by suspending a fluorescent workshop light over the plants. By using linked chains to support the light, you can adjust the height of the light so that it remains 5–10cm (2–4in) above the seedlings.

Avoid starting the seeds too soon, or you could find the seedlings will become too leggy and rootbound to transplant to a bed outdoors. For more about sowing seeds indoors see pages 64–65; for growing plants in a greenhouse see pages 78–81.

PLANTS TO START INDOORS

The following plants are among the best ones that you can start off indoors:

Broccoli	Cucumbers
Brussels sprouts	Leeks
Cabbage	Lettuce
Cauliflower	Onions
Chive	Tomatoes

Quick Tip

Light fantastic

If your row of cloches are within reach of an electrical socket, you can add extra warmth by running two lines of outdoor Christmas lights inside the row of cloches, one along each side. The heat from the bulbs lifts the temperature a few degrees.

Tunnels and frames

Structures in the vegetable garden such as tunnels and frames provide more facilities for raising tranplants – or even for growing crops until they reach maturity.

COLD-FRAME VEGETABLES

You can grow the following vegetables to maturity in a frame:

early carrots	cucumbers
winter lettuce	some melons
spring lettuce	

Quick Tip

Make a frame

You can build a frame using an old window from a reclamation centre. (If you're not sure if it has lead paint, apply a coat of an exterior paint.) Make the base from wood the size of the window, with a height of about 60cm (24in) at the back, sloping to 45cm (18in) at the front.

Sometimes plants growing in their permanent planting positions will need protection to help them survive a late frost in the spring or an early one in the autumn. The same methods for providing this type of protection can also be used to harden off transplants (see pages 68–69).

Tunnels

You can easily obtain tunnels made from polythene sheeting, which are versatile products for the garden. They are lightweight and simple to work with. Although they do not have a long life (two or three years), they are inexpensive to replace.

Polythene sheeting is often used to form long, low tunnels that are about 30–60cm (12–24in) high, and these can be used as a type of cloche (see page 75). You can easily construct a low tunnel yourself by driving a series of metal hoops into the ground, stretching the polythene over them and securing it in place with either twine or more metal hoops. Form the ends of a cloche by gathering together the polythene and tying it to a stake. To ventilate the tunnel simply push the polythene up along the sides.

You can create a tunnel for any size that is required, whether it is to cover a single row of seedlings or a whole patch of early lettuce crops – you can even construct it as a walk-in tunnel